Tucholsky Wagner Zola Scott Sydow Freud Schlegel
Turgenev Fonatne Wallace
Twain Walther von der Vogelweide Fouqué Friedrich II. von Preußen
Weber Freiligrath Frey
Kant Ernst
Fechner Fichte Weiße Rose von Fallersleben Richthofen Frommel
Hölderlin
Engels Fielding Eichendorff Tacitus Dumas
Fehrs Faber Flaubert
Eliasberg Ebner Eschenbach
Feuerbach Maximilian I. von Habsburg Fock Zweig
Ewald Eliot Vergil
Goethe Elisabeth von Österreich London
Mendelssohn Balzac Shakespeare Dostojewski Ganghofer
Trackl Lichtenberg Rathenau Doyle Gjellerup
Stevenson Tolstoi Hambruch
Mommsen Lenz Droste-Hülshoff
Thoma von Arnim Hanrieder
Dach Verne Hägele Hauff Humboldt
Karrillon Reuter Rousseau Hagen Hauptmann Gautier
Garschin Defoe Baudelaire
Damaschke Hebbel
Descartes Hegel Kussmaul Herder
Wolfram von Eschenbach Dickens Schopenhauer Rilke George
Bronner Darwin Melville Grimm Jerome
Campe Horváth Aristoteles Bebel Proust
Voltaire Federer
Bismarck Vigny Barlach Herodot
Gengenbach Heine
Storm Casanova Tersteegen Grillparzer Georgy
Chamberlain Lessing Langbein Gilm
Gryphius
Brentano Lafontaine
Strachwitz Claudius Schiller Kralik Iffland Sokrates
Bellamy Schilling
Katharina II. von Rußland Gerstäcker Raabe Gibbon Tschechow
Löns Hesse Hoffmann Gogol Wilde Vulpius
Luther Heym Hofmannsthal Gleim
Roth Klee Hölty Morgenstern Goedicke
Heyse Klopstock Kleist
Luxemburg Puschkin Homer Mörike
La Roche Horaz Musil
Machiavelli Kraft Kraus
Navarra Aurel Musset Kierkegaard
Nestroy Marie de France Lamprecht Kind Kirchhoff Hugo Moltke
Laotse Ipsen Liebknecht
Nietzsche Nansen Ringelnatz
Marx Lassalle Gorki Klett Leibniz
von Ossietzky May
Petalozzi vom Stein Lawrence Irving
Platon Knigge
Sachs Pückler Michelangelo Kafka
Poe Kock
Liebermann Korolenko
de Sade Praetorius Mistral Zetkin

The publishing house tredition has created the series **TREDITION CLASSICS**. It contains classical literature works from over two thousand years. Most of these titles have been out of print and off the bookstore shelves for decades.

The book series is intended to preserve the cultural legacy and to promote the timeless works of classical literature. As a reader of a **TREDITION CLASSICS** book, the reader supports the mission to save many of the amazing works of world literature from oblivion.

The symbol of **TREDITION CLASSICS** is Johannes Gutenberg (1400 – 1468), the inventor of movable type printing.

With the series, tredition intends to make thousands of international literature classics available in printed format again – worldwide.

All books are available at book retailers worldwide in paperback and in hardcover. For more information please visit: www.tredition.com

tredition was established in 2006 by Sandra Latusseck and Soenke Schulz. Based in Hamburg, Germany, tredition offers publishing solutions to authors and publishing houses, combined with worldwide distribution of printed and digital book content. tredition is uniquely positioned to enable authors and publishing houses to create books on their own terms and without conventional manufacturing risks.

For more information please visit: www.tredition.com

The Military Journals of Two Private Soldiers, 1758-1775 With Numerous Illustrative Notes

Abraham Tomlinson

Imprint

This book is part of the TREDITION CLASSICS series.

Author: Abraham Tomlinson
Cover design: toepferschumann, Berlin (Germany)

Publisher: tredition GmbH, Hamburg (Germany)
ISBN: 978-3-8491-8623-4

www.tredition.com
www.tredition.de

Copyright:
The content of this book is sourced from the public domain.

The intention of the TREDITION CLASSICS series is to make world literature in the public domain available in printed format. Literary enthusiasts and organizations worldwide have scanned and digitally edited the original texts. tredition has subsequently formatted and redesigned the content into a modern reading layout. Therefore, we cannot guarantee the exact reproduction of the original format of a particular historic edition. Please also note that no modifications have been made to the spelling, therefore it may differ from the orthography used today.

Ruins Of Fort Ticonderoga
(From Lossing's Field Book of the Revolution.)

ADVERTISEMENT.

(p. 005)

Having been, for several years, engaged in the establishment of a Museum in Poughkeepsie, I have, by extensive travel and research, and by the kindness of many of my fellow-citizens in Dutchess county and elsewhere, obtained numerous objects, not only curious in themselves, but valuable as materials for history. Among these are two manuscript Journals, kept by common soldiers, each during a single campaign, and written at periods seventeen years apart. One of these soldiers served in a campaign of the conflict known as the French and Indian War, which commenced a hundred years ago; the other soldier assisted in the siege of Boston, by the American army, in 1775 and 1776. Believing that a faithful transcript of those Journals, given *verbatim et literatim*, as recorded by the actors themselves, might have an interest for American readers, (p. 006) as exhibiting the every-day life of a common soldier in those wars which led to the founding of our republic, I have yielded to the solicitations of friends, and the dictates of my own judgment and feelings, and in the following pages present to the public faithful copies of those diaries.

Perceiving that much of the intrinsic value of these Journals would consist in a proper understanding of the historical facts to which allusions are made in them, I prevailed upon Mr. Lossing, the well-known author of the *"Pictorial Field-Book of the Revolution"* to illustrate and elucidate these diaries by explanatory notes. His name is a sufficient guaranty for their accuracy and general usefulness; and I flatter myself that this little volume will not only amuse, but edify, and that the useful objects aimed at in its publication will be fully attained. With this hope, it is submitted to my fellow-citizens.

Abraham Tomlinson.

Poughkeepsie Museum, *December, 1854.*

INTRODUCTORY REMARKS.

(p. 007)

The conflict known in America as the *French and Indian War*, and in Europe as the *Seven Years' War*, originated in disputes between the French and English colonists, in the New World, concerning territorial limits. For a century the colonies of the two nations had been gradually expanding and increasing in importance. The English, more than a million in number, occupied the seaboard from the Penobscot to the St. Mary's, a thousand miles in extent; all eastward of the great ranges of the Alleganies, and far northward toward the St. Lawrence. The French, not more than a hundred thousand strong, made settlements along the St. Lawrence, the shores of the great lakes, on the Mississippi and its tributaries, and upon the borders of the gulf of Mexico. They early founded Detroit, Kaskaskia, Vincennes, and New Orleans.

The English planted agricultural colonies—the French were chiefly engaged in traffic with the Indians. This trade, and the operations of the Jesuit missionaries, who were usually the self-denying pioneers of commerce in its penetration of the wilderness, gave (p. 008) the French great influence over the tribes of a vast extent of country lying in the rear of the English settlements.

The ancient quarrel between the two nations, originating far back in the feudal ages, and kept alive by subsequent collisions, burned vigorously in the bosoms of the respective colonists in America, where it was continually fed by frequent hostilities on frontier ground. They had ever regarded each other with extreme jealousy, for the prize before them was supreme rule in the New World. The trading-posts and missionary-stations of the French, in the far Northwest, and in the bosom of the dark wilderness, several hundred miles distant from the most remote settlements on the English frontier, attracted very little attention until they formed a part of more extensive operations. But when, after the capture of Louisburg, by the English, in 1745, the French adopted vigorous measures for opposing the extension of British power in America; when they built strong vessels at the foot of Lake Ontario—made treaties of friendship with powerful Indian tribes—strengthened their fort at the mouth of the Niagara river — and erected a cordon of fortifications, more than sixty in number, between Montreal and New Orleans, — the English were aroused to immediate and effective action in defence of the territorial limits given them in their ancient charters. By virtue of these, they claimed dominion westward to the Pacific ocean, south of the latitude of the north shore (p. 009) of Lake Erie; while the French claimed a title to all the territory watered by the Mississippi and its tributaries, under the more plausible plea that they had made the first explorations and settlements in that region. The claims of the real owner — the Indian — were lost sight of in the discussion; and it was a significant question asked by an Indian messenger of the agent of the English *Ohio Company*: "Where is the Indian's land? The English claim it all on one side of the river, and the French on the other: where does the Indian's land lie?"

The territorial question was brought to an issue when, in 1753, a company of English traders and settlers commenced exploring the head-waters of the Ohio. The French opposed their operations by force. George Washington was sent by the Virginia authorities to remonstrate with the French. It was of no avail. The English determined to oppose force to force; and in the vicinity of the now-flourishing city of Pittsburg, in western Pennsylvania, the "French and Indian War" began. Provincial troops were raised, and armies came from England. Extensive campaigns were planned, and attempts were made to expel the French from Lake Champlain and the southern shore of Lake Ontario. Finally, in 1758, three armies were in motion at one time against French posts remote from each other — Louisburg, in the extreme east; Ticonderoga, on Lake Champlain; and Fort Du Quesne, where Pittsburg now stands. General Sir James Abercrombie commanded (p. 010) the expedition against Ticonderoga, accompanied by young Lord Howe as his lieutenant. The French were under the command of the marquis Montcalm, who was killed at Quebec the following year. The English and provincial troops rendezvoused at the head of Lake George, went down that sheet of water, attacked Ticonderoga, and were repulsed with great loss. It was this portion of that campaign in which the soldier served who kept the Journal given in the succeeding pages. It is a graphic outline picture, in few and simple words, of the daily life of a common soldier at that time.

During the campaign of 1759, Quebec was captured by the army under Wolfe; Lord Amherst, more successful than Abercrombie, drove the French from Lake Champlain; Sir William Johnson captured Fort Niagara; and all Canada was in virtual possession of the English, except Montreal. That fell early in the Autumn of 1760; and the struggle for supremacy in America, between the French and English, was ended for ever.

L.

MILITARY JOURNAL FOR 1758.

(p. 011)

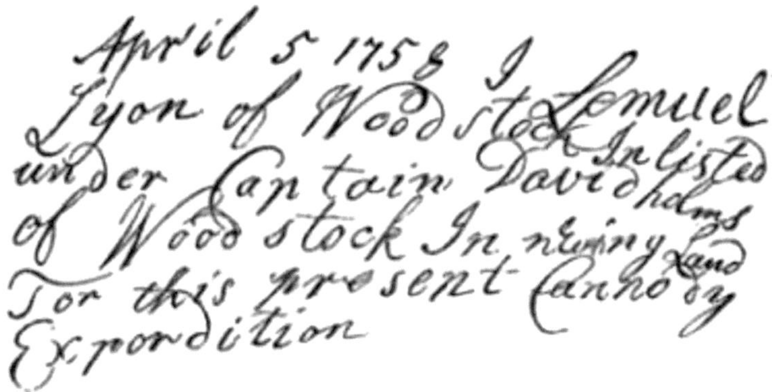

Fac-simile of a Portion of the Manuscript Journal.

April 5 1758. I Lemuel Lyon of Woodstock Inlisted under Captain David holms of Woodstock in newingLand For this present Cannody Expordition[1] — I Received of Captain Holms £2.0s.0d.

May 30. Received £3,-16-0.

June, 2nd. We arrived at Colonal Maysons at 12 o'Clock and marched from their to Landard[2] Abits & Sergent Stone treated us their — then we marched to mansfield to Deacon Eldridgs about four o'clock — then we (p. 012) marched to Bolton to Landard trils, and we gave 7d a night for horse keeping.

Wednesday 7th. We had Carts to press,[3] — then we marched of from their to Landard Strengs in Harford and from their to Landard Geds & had raw Pork for dinner — then we marched to Landard Crews and the Chief[4] lodges their — My mess lodged at a private house one Daniel Catlins.

Thursday 8th. Marched of and arived at Landard Gessels and their we went to Brecfirst and then we marched from their to our stores in Litchfield[5] to Squire Sheldings and then to Landard Buels and lodged their and our Captain was sent for to a man in another Company that had fits.

Friday 9th. Then marched from their and we had nu teams presed their and we arrived at Landard Hollobuts in Goshen from their to widow Leggets in Cornwell[6] and from their to Coles in Cainan[7] & lodged their.

Saturday 10th. Marched to Lawrences and from thence to Landard Bushes in Shefield 7 mile and went to diner—thence marched and arived at one Garnt Burges and lodged their and our Ensign went to Prayer with us—

Sonday (p. 013) 11th. Marched into the Paterroon Lands[8] to Landard Lovejoys & went to diner had a hard shower then marched into Cantihook[9] to one Hayer Carns the Stone house & lodged their & from thence to Cantihook Town to one Bushes and slept their.

Monday 12th. At Cantihook.

Tuesday 13th. Marched and arived at the half way house in Albany & Bated, & then into Green Bush[10] by Son down and lodged their in Ranslays Barn.

Wednesday 14th. Stil at Albany and their I first shifted my clothes and washed them—then we had 6 rounds of powder & ball & had orders from Colonel Whiting to go to Senakada[11]—this day Asel Carpenter came to Albany.

Thursday 15th. We went over the River Early to receive our rations in provision and in money and we marched 2 Miles and stoped and refreshed ourselves their half an hour and Lieut. Smith came up and we received our Abilitan money.[12]

Friday 16th. We had Prayers in our company at 3 Ock (p. 014) then all marched of but 14 and they stayed here to guard Lieut Smith and the money and yesterday Mr. Holmes sot of for Home and I giv 5 pence for carring my letter—we stayed here til 5 oclock this afternoon and we heard nothing from Lieut Smith and we had no provisions so we marched for Scanacata[13] and we got in at Son down well & their was a Larrom[14] this night.

Saturday 17th. Stil at Schenacata[15] and we moved into our Barrocks and Barnabas Evings was taken poor with a working in the Body Ben denny was taken very poor.

Sonday 18th. I was first called upon guard with 15 more. My turn came first at 11 oclock—this afternoon 3 ock Lieut. Smith come up with our abilitan money.

Monday 19th. Stil at Schenacata and their was a rigiment of province men[16] come up to Schenacata and this night 25 of our men went over the River west 1 mile to guard wagon Horses—this day a short training 1 Regiment.

Tuesday 20th. Their marched of 3 Hundred of the Bay Forces[17] for Fort Edward[18] and I received my abilitan in full £1.8s.0d.

Wednesday (p. 015) 21st. Stil hear and we were imbodied for prayers in the morning and then trained a little. Corperal Carpenter was taken poor.

Thursday 22d. Had orders to march to the half moon[19] and Captain Leneses company to & at 7 oclk we marched and arivd at Tess-ceune[20] and Lodged their at Landard Abraham Grotes.

Friday 23d. Marched in the rain and very gresy traviling it was and we Arivd at Teburth and from thence to the place cald Lowdins Ferry[21] to Landard Fungdors and from thence to the half moon & Lodged their.

Saturday 24th. I received a Letter from John at the half moon and from thence we marched & Arived at Stil Water[22] & Lodged their & Barnabas Evings was poor.

Sonday (p. 016) 25th. We got 2 Battoes[23] to carry our packs up to Salatogue[24] and we went a foot & 8 of our men were draun out to stay at Salatogue—Captain Lewis shot at an Indian and kild him & sot in the Battoe—from Salatogue we marched on to Fort Miller[25] and Lodged their.

Monday 26th. Rainy and wet—I come up the River in a Battoe to Fort Edward to the incampment—their we drad 1/2 a pound of powder and 10 Bullets a peace and 8 days provision in order for to march to the Lake[26]—Barnabas Evings was very poor with fever nago[27] and was forst to stay behind & David Bishop with him—we Lodged in Bush tents and very wet it was.

Tuesday (p. 017) 27th. Marched all of Colonel Phiches[28] Regiment that were hear with 3 teams to carry the officers we arrived at the half way Brook[29] and their a great percel stashond for a while & from thence we Marched to Lake George and went over upon the hill East & their Encamptt one with myself went upon guard this night.

Wednesday 28th. We cleard our ground and pitchd our tents I sent 2 letters home.

Thursday 29th. Stil here General Limon[30] & Colonel Phiches Regiments come up to the Lake this day I washed my Cloths 1 more rigiment come up.

Friday 30th. This day there was a very unhapy mishap fel out in the province forces & that was 1 **** shot one **** partly through the body but did not kil (p. 018) him the man which was shot lived at Bridgwater to day they drawd out 9 men to go in Battoes up the Lake.

Saturday July 1st. Colonel Worster[31] & his rigiment came up to day & 3 of our sick men 1 of them Brot nuse that one man shot another by accident at Schenacata & an hour after he died to day our Chapling[32] came up &. 1 of Magor Rogers[33] men came in that had bin (p. 019) gorn 7 days & Expected to be gorn but 2 he was so beat out that he could not tel what had becom of tother. this night I went upon a batto and guarded Colonel Phiches Tub of Butter.

Sonday 2. In the fore noon I went to meting & heard Mr. Eals his text was in the 5th Chapter of James 16th verse a good sermon I rote a letter & sent home & in the after noon to meeting again.

Monday 3d. Yesterday Mager putnoms S Company came up and this morning Mager putnom[34] come up and (p. 020) the Connetticuts rigiment were Imbodied for to learn how to form your front to the Right and left for Jineral Abbacromba[35] and his A de Camp to vieu.

Tuesday 4. This day I cut my hat and received my amanition and provision for 4 days and made radey for to go on.

Wednesday 5th. This day the Army by son rise got ready for to March and Marched of by Water, and Arived at the Saberday point[36] & stayed their til midnight then (p. 021) Marched again to the first narrows & Landed their and went down.

Thursday 6th. 12 A Clock at night we marched of again[37] & landed at the 1st narrows & then we Marched on to the falls[38] within 2 miles of the fort and there we was attackt by the Enemy[39] and the Engagement held 1 (p. 022) hour and we kiled and took upwards of 2 & 50, & of Captain Holmes Company we had 3 Men wounded. Sergent Cada Sergent Armsba and Ensign Robbins & at Sondown the French come out again 5 thousand strong and our men came back again to the Landing place & Lodged their.

Friday 7th. Majer Rogers went down to the mils and drove them of there from & kild and took upwards of 150 & at Son down the last of the Army marched down to the Mils and Majer putnom made a Bridge over by the Landing place this night we lodged by the Mils.

Saturday 8th. Then marched back 2 or 3 rigiments to the Landing place to guard & help Get up Artillira and we worked all the fore noon onloading the Battoes and at noon we set out down to the Mils with the Artillira & we got near the Mils and we had orders to leave the Artillira[40] their and go back & get our arms and (p. 023) we went down to the Mils of our rigiment 2 Hundred were ordered to go over on the point to keep the French from Landing their and we stayed while next morning son 2 hours high & when we came in all our army and Artillira was gorn back & the Mils fired and we marched back to the Landing place and had to secure matter of 200 Barrels of Flour & we heard the French were a coming upon us and we stove them all and come of us as soon as we could and about 10 Ock we sot sail and & by Son down we arrived at Lake George[41] according to all accounts the Engagement began about 10 clock and held 10 Hours steady and we lost 3 Thousand rigulars.

Monday 10th. Stil at Lake George in our old encampment 2 Cannon and 2 morter peaces all of them Brass come into Lake George to day.

Tuesday 11th. I washed my Clothes to day had Tea for Brecfirst.

Wednesday (p. 024) 12th. To day I was cald upon guard. Stephen Lyon went to Fort Edward.

Thursday 13th. To day washed My Clothes.

Friday 14th. Nothing remarkable.

Saturday 15th. Nothing remarkable cald out to work.

Sonday 16th. Went to meeting to hear Mr. Pommerai[42] & his text was in the 16th Chapter of Isaiah the 9th verce in the afternoon went to hear Mr. Eals and his text was in 4th Chapter of Amos & the 12th verce Sung the 45 Salm the last time sung the 44th Salm this day Colonel Dotays Rigiment marched of.

Monday 17th. This day Sergent Joseph Mathers had a new shirt put on of 70 stripes[43] I washed and at night was caled upon the picket guard Barny went down to the halfway brook[44] and back again to guard Artillira.

Tuesday 18th. One Samuel Jonson died very suddenly he belonged to Captain Latimer Company of new Cannen, Nehemiah Blackmore was whipt 10 stripes for fireing his gun.

Wednesday 19th. This day to work upon the Hospetal gitting timber to it I went upon the Island[45] to stay thair a week.

Thursday (p. 025) 20th. Stil at work Colonel Worster sot out to go down to Albany and a number of men with him this morning 10 Men were a going to the half way Brook to guard the Post and the Indians way laid them and kild 9 of them & 1 got in safe and they rallyd out from the Brook 100 & went back to see what was the Matter and they laid wait for them & they fired upon the front first and kiled 2 Captains and 2 Leiutenants on the spot & our men were supprised and run back all but a few and they stood a little while & lost 17 men the engagement began son 2 hours high about a nowr after Leiut. Smith & 200 of our men went down to help guard the teames down to Fort Edward.

Friday 21st. This day at knight Leiut. Smith came back & very poor he was the rest of the guard returned well.

Saturday 22d. This day Colonel Partrages[46] rigiment were resolved to have their full Allowance or go of and they got it[47]—a small shower & at night our post came in and our Men that stayed behind came up I received a letter from Home.

Sonday 23d. Went to meeting and the text was in the (p. 026) 3 chapter of John & the 16 verse & in the after noon the Text was in the 6 chapter of Micah 6 & 7 verses this day wet & hard showers.

Monday 24th. This day a week ago Ensign Robins died at Albany this day Henry Morris came up to Lake George with 2 Waggon Loads of Rum and sold it right of—

Tuesday 25th. Captain Holmes and 5 of our men went down to the half way Brook to be stashoned their til Furder orders—at 9 Ock one James Makmehoon[48] was hanged upon the galloes upon the top of the Rockka noose[49] our post came in and I was released from the Haspital work.

Wednesday 26th. Majer putnom had orders to list 400 ranjers and listed some to day.

Thursday 27th. This day the Captains of the Companys drawed out 9 men of a company for ranjers.

Friday 28th. There was about 40 teams & wagons a coming up about half way between Forte Edward and half way Brook and a scout of French & Indians way laid them and kiled every ox and destroyed all their stors every thing[50] and about midnight our camps were alarmd of it and Majer putnom rallyd about a 1000 Men & went after them.

Saturday 29th. This day Rogers went upon the track with (p. 027) his ranjers[51] and sent back for all the picket guard and they went & this day I was very poor & took a portion of fizik.

Sonday 30th. This morning by break of day som of Majer put-noms men that he left with the Battoes spied some more a coming down the Lake and they com & told & Limon rallyd up about 2000 men and went up the Lake I was poor and went to meeting Mr. Ingarson[52] preach'd & his text was in salms the 83 & the 14 & 15 & the after noon the text was in Duteronemy 32 & 29 verse.

Mon. 31st. 9 of our Newingland Men were put under guard for making a false larrom about the battoes coming down upon us & also one regular that Rogers took that desarted last year to the French from us.

Tuesday August 1st. Their was about 700 men went down to the Half Way Brook to be stashond their and 8 of our company and Captain Holmes came back.

Wednes. 2. To day Jineral Limon came in of a scout & the men that went with him and Rogers and putnom went of a scout with 14 or 15 hundred for 10 days[53] this day Craft died and was buried Stephen Lyon come of scout.

Thurs. (p. 028) 3rd. Two of our men went out a fishing for 2 days but had poor luck.

Friday 4th. We had orders to march to Fort Edward & I washed up my clothes.

Sat. 5th. This morning about half our rigiment marched forward to build brest Works along upon the road in some bad places we arived at Fort Edward at 9 O clock & we Built 2 Brest works.

Sonday 6th. We drawd 3 days provision and this afternoon the Rest of our Rigiment came down and the teams that went up the day Before we received our pacet[54] of letters from home.

Monday 7th. Cap.n & all that were able to go were ordered to guard down to Fort Miller and back again.

Tues. 8th. In the morning we were drawd out for work and worked the fore noon then we were ordered to fix every Man in the rigiments to make ready, to go out to help Majer putnom and we met them a coming in about son down and we helpt them a long as far as we could & that nite & lay out that nite & 3 of the wounded men died there and Ben Deny for one.[55]

Wed. (p. 029) 9th. We got in about 8 a clock & Buried the dead & the wounded were dresd & carried over on the Island[56] Powers came up with a load of Settlers[57] stores and treated us well.

Thur. 10th. I was cald out to work upon the Block house this day our post went of home with our letters.

Friday 11th. We went up to guard teams to Half Way Brook and to Build a Brest Work 36 Ox teams & 6 Wagons.

Sat. 12th. Colonel Phich[58] had a letter from Major putnom at tiantiroge[59] he is taken prisoner.[60]

Son. (p. 030) 13th. Day the chief of our men upon duty and the rest went to meeting the afternoon the text was in the 2nd of timothy the 1st chapter & 10 verce.

Mon. 14. I had nothing to du I rote a letter to John.

Tues. 15. I was upon picit[61] guard & wet and stormy it was 1 of the regalars whipt for sleping upon guard.

Wednesday 16. The ranjers discoverd a scout of French & com in to Fort Edward and all that were able were ready at a minits warning to day I sent a Letter to John Lyon.

Thursday 17th. w, p, 31 stripes stil & Nothing to do the Liev.ts fixed up their tents.

Friday 18th. 6 of our men were ordered to go over to work upon the Block House over the river I was raly tired at night.

Saturday 19th. I washed My clothes Col fitch at Salatogue.

Sonday 20th. We were almost all out upon duty to work at the High Ways and in the after noon a very hard shower which sot our tents all aflote.

Monday 21st. I went down to Fort Mizerey[62] & I heard (p. 031) of John Day's death at Saletogue this day Morris came up and we lived well.

Tuesday 22d. I went up the river to look for a horse Steven & I was cald upon picit guard.

Wednesday 23d. I went out to look oxen and was treated well 1 mans gun went of and cut of his finger we drove out the 2 men out of the Block House kep the great Cattle.

Thursday, 24th. I was cald out to guard up teams and to work on the road & had a Jil of rum for it Zachariah Catlin died at Fort Edward.

Friday 25th. I was cald upon the quorter guard & we heard the great guns that were fired at the Lake[63] they shot at a mark and our Provinshals beat them & it made them very mad.

Saturday 26. David Lyon and Barnes sot out to go to Albany sick this day they held a rigimental Court Mershal upon 3 deserters of Captain Mathers company one William Cannody & William Clemanon were Judged to have 1000 Lashes and to day receved 200 & 50 stripes a peace tother was forgiven.

Sonday 27. I was out upon the works at the great Block House we were out of provision we drawed for 7 days & but 4 gorn so the regalers shot Pigeons and our men did so to.

Monday 28th. Every Private in our company was out upon duty that was able, & about 4 a clock we came in and the orders were that every man should make (p. 032) ready to fire 3 valleys[64] and first they fired the cannon at the Fort one after tother round the Fort which is 21 then the small arms & so 3 rounds a piece and then made a great fire on the Perrade and played round it & 1 Jil of Rum a man aloud for the frollic & a Barrel of Beer for a Company[65] & very wet knight.

Tuesday 29th. Very wet in the Morning then cleared of cold I went upon duty and sent a Letter Home.

Friday September ye 1st. Our duty was to help git out the Cannon out of the Bottom of the river that was dropt in by the means of going to near the end of the Brig[66] and sunk the scows and drownd 1 ox very cold work A woman whipt 70 stripes & drumed out of Camp.

Saterday 2nd. I was cald upon the pickit guard to day last nite I went down to Fort Misketor[67] & Smith Ainsworth treated us well.

Sonday 3rd. I was out upon the escort and every man upon som duty I went to meeting part of the fore noon and the text was in acts 24 & 25 Charles Ripla was put in Ensign.

Monday 4th. Our Post sot of home I went down to Fort Misketor to guard teams and the Post and the Lobster's[68](p. 033) and our men hopt & rassled[69] together to see which would beat and our men Beat.

Tuesday 5th. Stil & Nothing strange.

Wednesday 6th. Most all of our men upon duty I was to work a making a road to go up to the great Block House.

Thursday 7th. All our men out upon works guardin teams a great number of them nigh 100 & when we came back their was a scout com in to Fort Edward that went out from the Lake they discoverd nothing.

Friday 8th. This day sergent Erls went out to Fort An[70] after the Con-nu[71] & Lieut. Larnard & Ephraim Ellinghood Knap & John Richason and Jeb Brooks & Hezekiah Carpenter they 6 of our company 40 in all (p. 034) went along I went to work at the high way & had half a pint of Rum for it.

Saterday 9th. I was warned a quarter guard and I changed with Moses Peak and went upon the Escort & got in by 12 a clock I was warned out to work but did not do much sergent Erls com in with his Con-nu — and the Jineral was much pleased with it.

Sonday 10. I was upon guard but went to meeting a part of the fore noon and the text was in the 24 of Acts & 25 verce & the Afternoon the text was in James the 6th & 12 verce.

Monday 11. I took 4 days provision & Josh Barrit and one ranjer with me & we went out near fort An and we spied a fire and som person and we com back and made our report to the Jeneral & he blamed us som and said we should have a new pilot and go again. Jo Downer put under guard.

Tuesday 12th. I was freed from duty and we went & split out som plank to du up our tent.

Wednesday 13th. To work in the Fort a wheeling gravel all day 4 regulars whipt in Fort som for gaming & one for being absent after being warned upon guard.

Thursday 14th. I was warned on Escort down to Mizzery[72] and flankt all the day Tuesday 12 at night there was 2 Bonfires & 2 Barrels of Rum aloud for the Rejoicing of Broad Street's taking Catarocrway.[73]

Friday (p. 035) 15th. Day I was to work over upon the Island & worked hard a shovling dirt &c Ephraim Ellinghood taken poorly.

Saturday 16th. Day I went to cuting fassheens[74] & stented 4 a peace in half a day & 12 stakes.

Sonday 17th. All our men upon works Mr. Pomri[75] preachd 1 sermon & his text in James Chapter 5th & 12 verce Stephen child had a post to Albany and sot out this day one regular com in that was a fishing at half way Brook.

Monday 18th. I was to work over to the Block House and took my Farewel of working their & all our sick were drawd up & som dischargd.

Tuesday 19th. 4 of our company had a final discharge from the Campain & sot of home Seth Bassit Jonathan Corbin John Peak & Silas Hoges.

Wednesday 20th. Stil Here the main of us & Nothing remarkable only almost all our woodstock men came up & with great Joy we recived them & much more the things that were sent us, I received a letter from Ben Lyon.

Thursday 21st. Nothing remarkable this day.

Friday 22nd. Our Woodstock Old melisha[76] sot out home & Lieutenant Smith & Corperal Peak & William Mercy & Samuel Leavins had a pass to Albany and went with them along down and Many more that did not Belong to our Company.

Saturday (p. 036) 23d. Our Post came up and I received a Letter from home.

Sonday 24th. Mr. Pomry[77] preachd one sermon in the middle of the day so that the work men might Have som opportunity to hear som his text was in Ezekiel the 37 Chapter & 36 verce I was to work upon the Island & I heard part of the sermon.[78]

Monday 25. Nothing remarkable only Stephen Lyon got hurt Samuel Morris & Chub went down along to Albany.

Tuesday 26th. One scout went out for 3 days this day a great number of teams came down from the Lake.

Wednesday 27th. The Thompson men that came up to see us sot out for newingland and sergent Cromba had a pass to Albany & went down along.

Thursday 28th. Nothing remarkable only the scout came in that went out for 3 days.

Friday 29th. Nothing remarkable only very long orders &c.

Saturday 30th. Nothing remarkable only the crissning[79] of the Royal Block House and the whole of our rigiment that were able went over to work and had a good frolick to drink the Men in

Jeneral worked well at the intrenching round the Block House the trench 3 foot deep.

Sonday (p. 037) October ye 1st. Nothing remarkable but somthing very strange, & that is the Camps were so stil and no work going foward nor no prayers nor no sermon & a Jil of Rum into the Bargain this we had from the Jenerals our month promised to us yesterday Mr. Pomri went down to Seratoga to see his son that was sick and to day he come back &c.

Monday ye 2nd. All the rigiment that were able to work went over to the Block House besides what wos upon guard and they were divided into 4 parties and they that got don first was to have the Best fat sheep 1 sheep to each party I was upon the grass Guard & at night I found it very tedious Lying out for it stormed exceding hard all night.

Tuesday ye 3rd. Our mes being all of duty we made us up 2 Straw bunks for 4 of us to lay in and as it hapened we did it in a good time for it was a very cold night.

Wednesday ye 4th. Being very cold Corperal Sanger & Eliezer Child had a pas down to Albany & Likewise a small scout went for Number four & we made our chimney serjant Kimbal was broke and turned into the ranks.

Thursday 5th. Jeneral Ambross[80] arrived at Fort Edward about 12 a clock & immediately he went of to the Lake nothing more remarkable to day.

Friday 6th. Henry Lyon and Ephraim Ellinghood poorly and cleared from duty 3 men whipt about 3 hundred (p. 038) lashes apeace & 1 woman 2 & 50 Lashes on bear rump.

Saterday 7th. Our Picket went up toward the Half way brook to meet jeneral Ambros[81] & about 3 a clock he arrived at Fort Edward and at 2 a clock the picket went down with him again and his wagon & 6 horses.

Sonday 8. In the fore noon all our men upon works in the afternoon we were aloud to attend meeting & Mr Pomy[82] Preached one sermon & his text was in Ezekiel 36 & 37 verce our family this day had a great rariryty for diner and that was a Bild Puden.

Monday 9. Nothing remarkable among us this day.

Tuesday 10. I was upon Guard and a very stormy day & Night it was orders came out strickt that all fires should be put out by 8 of the clock in the morning and not to have no more til 6 at night & they that dont obey the orders are to have their chimney tore down & not to have no other during this campaign Colonel Fitch lost a Barrel of wine.

Wednesday 11th. Stil warm & wet som of our Rigiment discharged Home but none of our company.

Thursday 12. A very clear cold morning all our men upon works & upon guard that were able Colonel Harts Rigiment of the Hampshier march down to Fort Edward in order for Home.

Friday 13th. All our men upon works again to day 3 dischargd vis Richard jordin, Stephen Lyon & John Howlet, (p. 039) at night 300 of the Bay men came down sick & 2 of them that carrad their packs died in the night.

Saturday 14th. All warned out upon works but the stormy wether defeted them in it the Regulars which came down from the Lake with us have orders to march next friday down along in order for their winter quorters at Hallefax[83] this night the sentry which stood at the Southerd of the store House spied a man a gitting of Flour and he haild him 3 times but he would not stop and the sentry fired but did not hit him & in his hurry he left his tom me hawk[84] & one shoe.

Sonday ye 15. Very cold all upon works & guard by son rise this evening their came in a great number of teams & Samuel Peak Brought the malancoly news of Stephen Childs being Kilde and skulpt[85] and another Captivated I was out upon the grass guard.

Monday 16th. All upon works & all the teams sot of for the Lake 12 men taken from the quorter guard to guard teams this evening there came in a great number of waggons and hundred or better.

Tuesday 17th. Being very pleasant in the Morning then showery & wet all the rest of the day til 10 a clock at knight — about 12 oclock at night the teams came in with the Artillira — this day a number of our men went down to Fort Miller in battoes to carry the sick and Cap.ns Bag went down & the men stayed out.

Wednesday 18th. Being cold the teams sot out for the Lake — about 40 of the Kings waggons — this afternoon their (p. 040) was a Lobster[86] Corperel married to a Road Island whore — our men came in from Fort Miller.

Thursday 19th. Our rigiment was mustered by 9 a clock in the morning & our Brigade-major cald over the role of each company and after that we had a drink of flip[87] for working over at the Royal Block House — at one of the clock our men were all calld to work — A Court morshol held at Capt. Holmes tent & Captain Holmes President & at the role of the Pickit guard their was one Isac Ellis whipt 30 stripes — was to had 50 — Col. Henmans[88] men came in loaded with Artillira stores.

Friday 20th. Cold stil & our men all upon works — this afternoon Lieut. Smith came up to us again from Green Bush, & Shubal child came to his team.

Saturday ye 21st. Still cold — in the morning our men cald out to work by sonrise or before & 6 of our company viz. David Bishop Ephraim Ellingwood Samuel Mercey Nathaniel Abbott David Jewet and Drake marched of with their Packs — this night their came down a great number of teams from ye Lake here loded with cannon Balls and Bum shells. Likewise a number of sick came down.

Sonday 22. The teams set out for ye Lake again — I was upon the quarter guard — a large number of sick (p. 041) sot out for Home & it yet held cold & at night it cleared of very clear & stil but very fresing cold & a black frost.

Monday ye 23rd. I come of guard — Clerk Burrows began his Month with bess — at night 3 rigiments of Province men came down from ye Lake & Lodged in the wood near the uper Block House — a number of teames down from ye Lake Loaded with Artilliry stores.

Tuesday 24th. A number of teames started for ye Lake again — I received 2 Letters from Capt. Benjamin Lyon & 1 from Joshua — the Post came up yesterday to Fort Edward — This day our drawing & we had good pork — 3 rigiments of Bay men moved down along which was Colonel Pribbels[89] Colonel Williams & Colonel Nichols.

Wednesday 25th. Jineral Abbacromba arived at Fort Edward near night and all our rigiment there were of duty were ordered to be out upon the perrade with their side arms on but the jineral for Bid it—Col.l Partrages rigiment came down & some of the Lather caps & stayed Here.

Thursday ye 26th. Stormy morning—snow pretty wet & raw cold—I went upon the pickit last night and had one Quort of rum for keeping sheep.

Friday 27th. Being lowry & wet one of our men Discharged home & sot of—Nathaniel Barnes a number of teams sot out for the Brook & returned again before son down.

Saterday (p. 042) 28th. Being stil cold all our men turned out to work son rise & that want a Nuf & they sent for every weighter[90] & every one that belongs to the rigiment—a number of teams sot out down Home ward & 3 of our company went with them viz. Sergt. Armsba Jonathan Child and Pain Convis—this after noon the orders came out that every setler[91] that Belongs to the Provinshols should Quit this place by the first of November.

Sonday ye 29th. Rany & wet—about 9 o clock in the morning Every man in the Rigiment that could go went to the falls[92] to help Draw down the battoes and very muddy it was.

Monday ye 30th. Being very pleasant in the morning we were all turned out after Battoes up to the falls & we went twice apeace.

Tuesday ye 31st. All our men turned out by the Revallies[93] Beating to go after Battoes & jineral Provorce[94] was out amongst our tents to help turn us out & he said it was the last work we should do that was flung up to day—I went upon the Quarter guard at noon and they got down all the Battoes.

Wednesday November ye 1st. Lowry & wet I come of guard our men all upon works & 3 rigiments of our Conneticuts came down about noon & Colonel Whitings had orders to go over to the Royal Block House and (p. 043) their to remain til further orders and tother 2 rigiments Sot of Home in Battoes & 2 or 3 rigiments of lobsters—we had orders com out that we should have 2 days to clean up in & to set for Home on Sonday—this day I wrote a Letter & sent to John.

Thursday ye 2nd. Very cold—our men turned out to cutting fashheens & the orders were that it was the last days work that we should do.

Friday ye 3d. Very cold—our men all turned out upon works notwith Standing yesterdays promise—our men had but poor incouragements to work & laid but Little weight to what the jineral promised them for he said the first man that disobeyed his orders again should be shot to death whatsoever soldier or officer.

Saturday 4th. I was orderly after the jineral & our men all to work a drawing in Canon into the fort & our quorter guard was not releaved til after noon & after that orders com out that we should strike our tents by 8 oclock and be ready to march by 9—one Cimbals got his discharge from the regular service to day.

Sonday ye 5th. Being very cold it began to rain so that we were detained but Colonel Whiting Marched of—rainy all day Long—we had orders to be ready to march at 7 Oclock in the morning.

Monday ye 6th. Cloudy stil—at 8 Oclock we struck our tents & at 9 aclock we marched of & about half after 12 we arrivd at Fort Miller and made a little stop then marched again and arived at Saratoga Son about one (p. 044) hour high & made no stop their but marched on about 3 mile & Encampt in the woods.

Friday ye 10th. Very stormy & snow in the Morning—we drawd 2 days alowance of provissions but no money and about 2 o clock we sot out from Green Bush & arivd at Cantihook Town about ten a clock at knight—13 of us & Lieutenant Larnard.

Saturday 11th. From thence we marched son two Hours high & arivd at John Hug gar Booms[95] & revived our selves a little & bought som rum that belonged to Colonel Whitens Rigiment & from thence to Love Joys & went to supper & from thence to Robberses & lodged their in the Patterroon lands.[96]

Sonday 12th. Being stil cold we sot out at Son rise & arived at Bushes in Sheffield and had a good brecfirst & their was moore with

Horses & from thence to Larrances & revivd our selves their—to Coles & thence to Seggick in Cornwel & then to Wilcocks in Goshen & Lodged their.

Monday 13th. Cold—I com up to Holleboate & sent my Pack a long from goshen & then we marched and arived at Litchfield & then to Herrintown to Wiers & from their to Strongs in Farming-town & Lodged their.

Tuesday 14th. Very cold & frosty—marched 5 mile through the Meadows & went to Brecfast and com to Mercies and stayed their & capt.n Holmes came up.

Wednesday 15th. We marched & arived at Chenys in Bolton and from thence we marched and Arived at Lees (p. 045) in covantry[97] & Lodged their—very rainy Stephen Lyon met us with the Horses.

Thursday 16th. Being warm & pleasant we arived at Woodstock.

Note.—The soldiers had, necessarily, a great deal of leisure during permanent camp-duties, and contrived various ways to amuse themselves, and "kill time." In those days the common soldiers carried their powder in the horns of cows or oxen, and many amused themselves by ornamenting them by a skilful use of their knives. Below is a specimen of one of these ornamented horns, prepared during the campaign of 1758. Upon it is neatly cut the figure of a fortified building (a part of which is seen in the engraving), the owner's name, and a verse, as follows:—

"Eluathan Ives His Horn, Made at Lake George, September ye 22d, Ad. 1758.

"I, powder, With My Brother Baul
A Hero like do Conquer All.
Steel not this Horn For Fear of Shame
For on it is the Oners name.
The Roos is Red, the Grass is Green—
The Days Are past Which I Have Seen"

(p. 047)

A JOURNAL FOR 1775, A. D.

INTRODUCTORY REMARKS.

(p. 049)

The following is a literal transcript of a Journal kept by a common soldier named Samuel Haws, of Wrentham, Massachusetts, who appears to have been one of the *minute-men*, organized toward the close of 1774 and early in 1775. At that time there were about three thousand British troops in Boston, under General Thomas Gage, who was also governor of the colony of Massachusetts. He was popularly regarded as an oppressor; and act after act of the British government, during a year preceding, had convinced the American people that they must choose the alternative to submit or fight. They resolved to fight, if necessary. During the summer of 1774, the people commenced arming, and training themselves in military exercises; the manufacture of arms and gunpowder was encouraged; and throughout Massachusetts, in particular, the people were enrolled in companies, and prepared to take up arms at a moment's warning. From this circumstance they were called "Minute-Men."

With his strong force, Gage felt quite certain that he could suppress the threatened insurrection, and keep the people quiet. Yet he felt uneasy concerning the gathering of ammunition and stores by the patriots at Concord, sixteen miles from Boston; and on the night of (p. 050) the 18th of April, 1775, he sent a detachment of soldiers to seize them. They proceeded by the way of Lexington, where they arrived at dawn of the 19th. The expedition became known, and the country was aroused. When the British approached Lexington, they were confronted by about seventy minute-men. A skirmish ensued: eight patriots were killed, and several were wounded. *That was the first bloodshed of the Revolution.* The British then went on to Concord, to seize the stores, where they were again confronted by minute-men. Indeed, they had been annoyed all the way by them, as they fired from behind buildings, stone-walls, and trees. They destroyed the stores, and in a skirmish killed several more American citizens. The country was now thoroughly aroused, and the minute-men hastened toward Lexington and Concord from all directions. The British found it necessary to retreat, and nothing saved the whole troop sent out the night before from utter destruction, but a strong reinforcement under Lord Percy. The whole body retreated hastily to Charlestown, and across to Boston, with a loss, in killed and wounded, of two hundred and seventy-three men. Intelligence of the tragedy soon spread over the country, and from the hills and valleys of New England thousands of men, armed and unarmed, hastened toward Boston, and formed that force (of which our Journalist was one) that, for nine months, kept the British army prisoners upon the peninsulas of Boston and Charlestown. By common consent, Artemas Ward, a soldier of the French and Indian war, was made commander-in-chief, and he performed the duties of that office with zeal until he was superseded by Washington, early in July, 1775.

A JOURNAL FOR 1775.

(p. 051)

Fac-simile of a Portion of the Manuscript Journal.

Wrentham,[98] April the 19.

About one a clock the minute men[99] were alarmed and met at Landlord Moons We marched from there the sun about half an our high towards Roxbury for we heard that the regulars had gone out and had killed six men and had wounded Some more that was at Lexinton then the kings troops proceded to concord and there they were Defeated and Drove Back fiting as they went they gat to charlstown hill that night[100] We marched to headens at Walpole[101] and their got a little refreshment (p. 052) and from their we marched to Doctor cheneys and their we got some victuals and Drink and from thence we marched to Landlord clises at Dedham[102] and their captain parson and company joined us and then we marched to Jays and their captain Boyd and company joined us and we marched to Landlord Whitings we taried their about one hour and then we marched to richardes and Searched the house and found Ebenezer aldis and one pery who we supposed to Be torys and we searched them and found Several Letters about them which they were a going to cary to Nathan aldis in Boston but makeing them promis reformation We let them go home then marching forward we met colonel graton[103] returning from the engagement which was the Day before and he Said that he would be with us amediately then we marched to Jamicai plain[104] their we heard that the regulars Were a coming over the neck[105] then we striped of our coats and (p. 053) marched on with good courage to Colonel Williams and their we heard to the contrary We staid their some time and refreshed our Selves and then marched to Roxbury parade and their we had as much Liquor as we wanted and every man drawd three Biscuit which were taken from the regulars[106] the day before which were hard enough for flints We lay on our arms until towards night and then we repaired to Mr. Slaks house and at night Six men were draughted out for the main guard nothing strange that night.

D 21. Nothing remarkable this day.

D 22. Nothing Strange this D nor comical.

D 23. Being Sabath day we marched on to the parade their was an alarm this night but it prouved to be a falce one Some of our men went to Weymoth.[107]

D 24. Nothing strange to day.

D 25. Nothing remarkable to day.

D 26. We were guarded and a party draughted out for the mane guard.

D 27. The inlistment came out to inlist men for the masechusetts Service Some of our minute men inlisted the Same day but captain Pond went home and several of his company they went as far as Doctor cheanys that night and the next morning reached home on monday the company were called together in order to inlist men Lietunant messenger with a party went down (p. 054) to Roxbury and we Still remaing in Mr. Slaks house also on the same day their war four tories caried throug roxbury[108] to cambrigg[109] from marshfield[110] and their was a great Shouting when they came through the camp.[111]

D 28. This day our regement paraded and went through the manuel exesise then we grounded our firelocks and every man set down by their arms and one abial Petty axedently discharged his peace and shot two Balls through the Body of one asa cheany through his Left side and rite rist he Lived about 24 hours and then expired he belonged to Walpole[112] and he was caried their and Buried on the 30 day of April on Sunday after meting this young man was but a few days Before fired at by one main guard in atempting to pass the guard and was not hurt in the least.

D 29. About nine o clock the said cheney died about fore in the afternoon We had another alarm but their was nothing done.

30th. Being the Lord's day we went to meeting and heard Mr. Adams[113] and he preached a very Sutable Sermon for the ocation.

May. (p. 055)

1d. Nothing very remarkable this day.

2d-11. Nothing of consequence hapened.

12-14. No great for news.

15, 16. No news worth mentioning.

17. At night their was a fire broke out in Boston ocationed by the kings troops that were a dealing out their Stores when one of the Soldiers letting a candle fall amongst some powder and set it on fire which ocationed the Destruction of a great number of Buildings and killed some Soldiers and destroyed a considerable deal of their amunition Besides a great quantity of flower.

18, 19. Nothing very remarkable.

20. Nothing strange to day.

21. Being Sunday about eight o clock we were alarmed we heard that the regulars were a landing at Dorchester Point and that there was two Lighters gone to Weymoth Loaded with the Kings troops but it was a false alarm and their was nothing done.[114]

22. (p. 056) Nothing to day for news.

23-26. Nothing remarkable.

the 27. At night we heard the report of cannon and of Small arms but we could not tell from whence it was.[115]

the 28. Being Sunday we were informed that the firing we heard yesterday was at Nedlers[116] Island between the Kings troops and our men, our men killed several of them and took a number of field pieces and burnt two Schooners and they did not hurt any of our men.

the 29. Nothing remarkable this day.

the 30. Captain Ponds company moved to comodore Lorings house.[117]

the (p. 057) 31. Being election day we drank the Ladies health and success.

June the 1. Nothing remarkable hapened this day.

the 2-8. Nothing remarkable hapened.

the 9. We passed muster Before colonel Robinson[118] and received one months pay.

the 10. Their was a man Whiped for Stealing.

the 11. Their was a soldier died at the hospittle which was the first that had died of Sickness since we incampt the same day their was two fire Ships[119] drumed out of the rhodisland compy.

the 12. Nothing Strange this day.

the 13. Dito.

the 14. The general[120] seing the reinforcement of the Kings troops come to Boston ordered the comps to be in readeness also ordered that a number of teams be imploid in carting fusheens[121] and other materials for building Brest Works this being on thursday.

the (p. 058) 15. Nothing remarkable this day.

the 16. Nothing of consiquence this day.

the 17. It being Saturday the Kings troops Landed at charlestown and set the whole town on fire and Laid it all in ashes then they proceeded to Bunkers hill[122] where colonel putnam intrenchet and after an engagement which Lasted the afternoon the troops took the Hill and it is said that the nearest computation of the Loss of the enemy was about 1500 is killed and wounded were alarmed about one o clock that day and went down to our alarm post and we lay their all the afternoon and about six o clock the troops fired from their Brest Work on Boston neck at our people in Roxbury and we staid until the firing was over and then our regiment was ordered to cambridge to asist our forces and we reached their about twelve o clock at night and Lodged in the meting house until break of day being Sunday (p. 059) we turned out and marched to prosket hill[123] expecting to come to an ingagement we halted at a house at the bottom of the hill and fixed for a battle then we marched up the hill where we went to intrenching about 12 o clock Some of our men went down the hill towards the troops after Some flower and the troops fired at them and wounded David Trisdale in the shoulder and another in the Leg about 4 o clock colonel Reed[124] ordered his regiment to march to roxbury and we arived their about sunset very weary.

the 19. Nothing remarkable this day.

the 20. Dito.

the 21. Nothing worth a mentioning.

the 22. Dito.

the 23. Nothing remarkable to day.

the 24. The enemy fired again upon Roxbury about 3 o clock and the guards fired upon each other and their was one man killed and we were alarmed.[125]

the (p. 060) 25. Sunday Nothing remarkable.

the 26. This morning very early our men went to set Browns house on fire but did not efect it.[126]

the 27. Nothing remarkable this day.

the 28. We moved to a little house that capt Bligs formerly Lived in but we Soon moved from there to Slaks house again.

the 29. Nothing remarkable this day.

the 30. Nothing hapened only there was a Smart shower.

July.

the 1. Nothing remarkable this day.

the 2. Dito.[127]

the 3. Dito.[128]

the 4. Their was a flag of truce come out of town to our centry on the neck.

the 5. Nothing worth a mentioning to day.

the 6. Nothing remarkable this day.

the 7. Early in the morning we were alarmed and all of us repaired to our alarm Post and we had not been (p. 061) their Long before we Saw Browns house and Barn on fire and they were both consumed[129] these were Set on fire by some of our brave ameracans and they took one gun and too Bagonets and one halbert.

the 8, 9. Nothing remarkable.

the 10. About Eleven o clock their was a party of Soldier sent to germantown[130] to get some whale Boats they marched down their that night the next night being clear they set out for Long island and arived there in a Short time then they Plundred the island and took from thence 19 head of horned cattle and a number of Sheep and three Swine[131] also eighteen priseners and amongst them were three women.

the 11. Nothing remarkable this day.

the 12. Major Tupper and his company returned to Roxbury with their prisoners and the same day their was a Party draughted out to go to Long island to burn the Buildings their when they were atacked by the Kings troops and had a smart engagement[132] but we Lost (p. 062) but one man and he belonged to Captain Persons company of Stoughton.[133]

the 13. Nothing remarkable this day.

the 14. Nothing remarkable untill night and then their was a man killed at the main guard with a canon Ball.

the 15-17. Nothing remarkable.

the 18. Nothing remarkable this day.[134]

the 19. We had an alarm and we went to our alarm Post and stayed their about one hour and could not discover any thing and so we returned to our Baracks again.

the 20. Their was a man killed who belonged to captain Bachelors company in Col Reeds Regiment he was killed by a guns going accidentely of, he was shot about Seven o clock and died about nine o clock the same night his name was Wood Belonged to upton[135] he was about 24 or 25 years of age.[136]

the 21-24. Nothing remarkable.

the 25. Our Regement with four more were under arms and marched towards cambridg to meet general Ward.

the 26. General Heaths regement moved from Dorchester to (p. 063) cambridg and Jeneral Wards regement moved from cambridg to Dorchester and took general Heath's Baracks.

the 27. Nothing remarkable this day.

the 28. Dito.

the 29. Nothing bad.

the 30. Being Sunday we had an alarm and went to our Fort[137] the same day there was a party of men draughted out to go to the Light house and major tupper was comander of the party.[138]

the 31. This day major tupper and his men returned to Roxbury with between thirty and forty prisoners some regulars and some torys and some mariens[139] and had something of a battle and we lost one man and another wounded and our men Burnt the Light house and took some plunder[140] thar was an alarm the firing began first (p. 064) at the floating Battery and then at the Brest Work and then the troops marched out and set the george tavern[141] on fire our men took one prisoner and the same night one of the enemy deserted and came to our centrys at Dorchester point and brought away with him too guns and too cartridg Boxes and 60 rounds of cartridgs all in good order and their was several more deserted to cambridg the same night.

August Domina 1775.

the 1. The floating Battery[142] went up towards Brookline fort[143] then our men perceiving her move they began to fire at her out of colonel Reeds fort untill they drove her back to her old place the same day they fired from Roxbury hill fort and it was said that they fired through their Baracks.

the 2. Nothing remarkable this day.

the 3. Dito.

the 4. Nothing remarkable to day only I went to the main guard and the enemy fired at us as we came up.

the 5. Dito.

the 6. Being Sunday nothing remarkable at night I went on the piquet guard.

the (p. 065) 7. Nothing strange.

the 8. Dito.

the 9. Nothing remarkable this day only I went upon fatigue.

the 10. Nothing strange We had a great rain.

the 11. Their was three men whipt for deserting they were whipt ten stripes apiece they belonged to the conecticut forces.

the 12. Nothing remarkable to day I went upon fatigue to Dorchester.[144]

the 13. Being Sunday we went to Hear Mr. Willard[145] and after Meting our Men went to Entrench down at the George tavern and About Brake of day they got Hom.

14. Their was Nothing Remarcable I went upon fatigue down to the George tavern.

15. Two Oclock this Afternoon when the Lobsters[146] fired on our guards which was returned by our Roxbury fort the fireing was continued for some time but how much to their Damag we dont know one of our men was slitely wounded their fireing was from a

floating Batery and it is thought would have killed one or too men if they had not have Lain down for the Ball passed (p. 066) within about 4 foot of our Barack the night passed without any alarm.

the 16. This day they fired at our main guard but no material Damage was done the remaining part of their mallice seemed to be postponed to a future season our american guard kept their ground and the night passed without any alarm &c. &c.

the 17. About nine Oclock the enemy fired upon our main guard and fatigue men they through 4 Balls and 2 Bombs and one of the Balls struck 2 guns which belonged to the main guard and the men had them on their Shoulders but did not hurt them much.

the 18. Behold their Spite this morning before the sun rise the enemy fired at our working party on the neck this side the george tavern our rifle men fired at them and it is thought killed too of them but notwithstanding all their fireing of balls and bombs though some of them came so near that it could hardly be called an escape yet their was not one man wounded on our side one bomb was thrown in the evening but did no Damage one of the enemy came to our centrys and is now in our guard house.

the 19. I went upon fatigue the morning began with fireing from the wicked enemy at our guard but did no hurt in the afternoon they rifle men fired at the enemy and they enemy at them and they wounded one of the rifle men in the foot Slitely but what Damage we did them is uncertain let this Suffice for a short acount of the tranactions of the 19 day.

the (p. 067) 20. I went upon the main guard at night our boats went up with in gun Shot of the comon[147] and alarmed them by fireing Several guns and then returned without any Loss on our side.

the 21. Nothing remarkable hapened this day at night one of the enemy deserted and came to us.

the 22. We paraded nothing remarkable I went down to the piquet.

the 23, 24. Nothing remarkable.

the 25. A flag of truce came out of town but for what I dont know.

the 26. This morning their was a man ran away from the floating battery.

the 27. Being Sunday but they make such a fireing over at Bunkers hill that it seems to be more Like the Kings birth day than Sunday but what Sucksess they have had we are not able to determine but we heard that they killed too men and wounded 3 or 4 four more[148]

the 28. But they still hold up their firing at Bunkers hill nothing more remarkable this day.

the 29. I went upon the piquet down to the george tavern and the enemy fired several small arms at us but did us no Damage.

the (p. 068) 30. Very rainy nothing extraordinary this day.

the 31. Nothing extraordinary this day only it was rainy at night Lieutenant Foster and four men went down to the piquet.[149]

Septem.

the 1. This morning very early just past one o clock the enemy began to fire from their Brest Work and their floating batery which ocationed an alarm their fireing Semed to be at our main guard and piquet they fired a number of guns and threw several bombs and they were permitted to kill too men the one belongd to Col Huntingtons[150] Regement and the other belonged to (p. 069) col Davidsons Regement and one of the riflemen was slitely wounded but see the Providence of god in it when 6 or 7 hundred men were before the mouths of their canon there was but too men killed We should not have thought it strange if they had killed 20 considering the Situation that they were in too of the regulars centrys deserted about a hour before the firing began this was the smartest fireing that ever has been this campaign in the afternoon they fired upon our fatigue party but did no Damage also about Sunset there was several guns fired on board the Ships there was several Ships came in to the harbour thus far the proceding of the 1 day.

the 2. I went down to the right hand of the burying place and we had not been their Long before we were ordered of and the canon began to play upon the enemy from Roxbury fort on the hill and the field peices from the brest work in the thicket the ocation of our mens fireing upon them was this they had advanced about 30 or 40 rods this side their other brest work on the neck and were intrenching their[151] they fired several guns at us but did us no Damage in the afternoon we went down to our work again expecting every moment when they would fire at us but they never fired one gun in the afternoon at night thir was a platform caried down to the thicket in order to mount a canon their Nothing more remarkable to day.

the (p. 070) 3. Being Sunday we turned out about day and went to our alarm post and it rained and we cam home and John coleman drinkt 3 pints cyder at one draught nothing more remarkable this day.

the 4. We turned out this morning before day and went to our alarm post nothing remarkable this day at night I went upon the piquet down to Lambs Dam[152] nothing more remarkable.

the 5. Nothing remarkable only Benjamin Mc Lain sent home 10 Letters at one draught by Lieutenant Bacon and Lieutenant Foster had Likt to have been put under guard for playing ball.

the 6. Nothing remarkable this day at Night our men went down below the george tavern for a safe guard for the centrys.

the 7. We turned out early this morning and went to our alarm post and had a smart scrimmage[153] with no enemy and this day I went upon the creek guard several Ships sailed out of the harbour old White was buried and their was much joy.[154]

the 8. Came of the creek guard and nothing remarkable hapned onely they enemy fired at our fatigue party but did no damage at night upon the door guard.

the 9. In the morning the enemy fired upon our fatigue party but did them no Damage in the afternoon I (p. 071) went upon fatigue at night our men caried Several canon down into the thicket to the brest works their.[155]

the 10. Being Sunday our men went on fatigue and the enemy fired upon them and broke three guns that were paraded but hurt no man at night their was a man deserted from cambridg and went to the enemy.

the 11. We turned out and went to our alarm post and Ensign Parot shook one of his men for disobying orders this day their was a boat drove ashore belonging to the regulars and a Seargent and 5 men on board and they were all taken prisoners at night I went upon the piquet and was almost frozen to Death.

the 12. Our men went down to Lambs Dam to entrenching not above half a mile from the enemys brest work but nothing remarkable hapened.

the 13. Colonel Clap officer of the day our men took this day 26 prisoners in mistick[156] river as we heard.

the 14. This morning I went upon fatigue down in the Street[157] and the enemy fired one shot at us and struck the brest work but did no Damage captain Pond[158] comanded of the party.

the 15. Their was a regular and too men of wars men[159] ran away Last night and this morning nothing more (p. 072) remarkable their was 3 guns fired on board the Ship in cambridg Bay.

the 16. Nothing remarkable hapened only the regulars fired several Shot at our men that were upon fatigue but did no Damage.

the 17. Being Sunday I went upon the fatigue and the enemy fired several times at our men but did no Damage and they threw several Bombs.

the 18. I came of the creek guard and the enemy fired several canon at our men but killed none and onely wounded one or too slitely and Last night their was several men ran away from a man of war and toward night the enemy fired several Shots from the Ship in cambridg bay and our men fired one Shot from Prospect hill at the Ship in the Bay but did not strike her.

the 19. The enemy began to fire about eight oclock into the street but did no damage except slitely wounding one or too at night I went upon the piquet and Nothing remarkable hapened also their was a man put under guard for comeing on to the parade Drunk.

the 20. Nothing remarkable hapened this day the enemy fired one shot at our fatigue party but did no damage they fired over at Bunkers hill and threw several Bombs.

the 21. Last night I was on the door guard and this morning the enemy fired small arms at our men but did no Damage in the afternoon they fired canon but to no purpose.

the (p. 073) 22. Last night I was upon the door guard this being the Kings crownation[160] the enemy fired a number of canon and toward night they put in balls but did no damage.

the 23. I went upon fatigue down in the street and the Enemy began to fire at us about 9 oclock and fired without intermition for some time bie the best acounts they fired above one hundred balls and our men fired 3 canon from our brest work near Lams Damb and one of the balls went into Boston amongst the housen but through the good hand of Devine providence in all their firing they did not kill one man nor wound any except one or too slitely.[161]

the 24. Being Sunday we went to meting and heard a fine Sermon from psalms 14-11 this day our men went on fatigue as usual but the enemy did not fire upon them.

the 25. I went on fatigue down in the thicket in the forenoon and at noon I was taken not well and did not go in the afternoon our men fired three field peices at the enemy but what execution they did we canot determine nothing more.

the 26. Nothing remarkable hapened this day onely their was 200 men draughted out to go to the governors Island to take some cattle.

the (p. 074) 27. Our men went to the Island and took 12 head of Cattle and 2 horses and came of without any Molestation[162] at night I went upon the piquet and it rained very hard and we turnd in to the housen and La their Colonel Clap[163] was officer of the piquet.

the 28. Nothing remarkable hapened this day there was too guns fired from the ship in Cambrige Bay.

the 29. This day the Ship sailed out of cambridge Bay and their was another came and took her place at night I went on the piquet without any supper nothing remarkable.

the 30. This morning our men fired one field peice as the regulars came to relieve their main guard and that afronted them and they began to fire their canon from their brest work and floating Batry and they fired about 30 canon but did no damage also last night their was too regulars deserted and came to our centrys on the neck nothing more remarkable this day.

October A 1775.

the 1. Being Sunday I went to meting up to the conecticut forces and Mr. Wilard preacht a Sermon from chronicles the 20th chapter 10-11-12 v also in the afternoon Mr. Wilard preachd a sermon from 1st of corrintheans 15 ch 54 &. 55 vers, also Last night their was (p. 075) six mareens dessrtd from on board the Scarborough.[164]

the 2. Nothing remarkable hapned this day General Thomas Brigade passt Mustter about Sunset as our piquet paraded on the grand parade the enemy fired 3 or 4 shots up to the meeting house one of the balls went through the shed by the Providence tavern but did no damage of consequence at night our chimney Swallow went on the piquet for nothing and found himself.

the 3. Nothing remarkable hapened this day at night I went upon the piquet.

the 4. We past muster nothing remarkble hapened this day onely their was four of the enemy deserted at night.

the 5. Nothing remarkable hapened this day onely their was 5 or 6 prisoners went through the camp that were taken at Dartmouth[165] on board the prize that our men took.

the 6. The enemy fired between 80 and 90 Canon at our men but killed nine onely cut of one mans arm and killed too cows So much for this day.

the 7. I went upon the creek guard and nothing remarkable hapned at night their was a regular deserted and (p. 076) the regular guard fired upon him but did not hurt him.

the 8. Being Sunday it rained and we had no preaching nothing remarkable hapned at night their was a regular deserted and came to our men and their was another set out but they were discovered and they took one of them.

the 9. About eight o clock their was a Rifle man whipt 39 stripes for Stealing and afterwards he was Drummed out of the camps if the infernal regions had ben opened and cain and Judas and Sam Haws[166] had been present their could not have ben a biger uproar.

the 10. I went up on the creek guard and nothing remarkable hapened their.

the 11. Their was a Rifle man[167] Drummed out of the camps for threatning his offisers also I went to Cambridg with Boats.

the 12. This day nothing remarkable hapned only I went to work along with the general at Mr. Parkers at night I went upon the piquet.

the (p. 077) 13. I went a chesnuting with a number of respectable gentlemen that belonged to the army and we had a rifle frolick[168] and came home about 10 Oclock.

the 13. About 2 or 3 o clock their was one of our men taken and caried to the quarter guard for thieft abel Weatheril by name but it was made up and he was taken out at night and returned to his Duty.

the 14. This day nothing remarkable hapned.

the 15. Being Sunday I went upon fatigue down to the george tavern and their was a flag of truce went in and another came out.[169]

the 16. Nothing remarkable hapned Colonel Reeds Laidy came down to reveu the Regiment and treated them[170] nothing more this day.

the 17. I went a chesnuting up to neutown[171] and at night our floating Baterys went up towards the canon and fired 13 shots but unlucky for them one of their 9 pounders split and killed one man dead and wounded 8 more one of them it is thought mortally.

the 18. I went upon the creek guard and John Bates was Lanch corporeal also in the afternoon their was 3 Boston (p. 078) men came out under pretence of fishing but they made their escape to Dorchester point.

the 19. Was rainy and nothing remarkable hapned.

the 20. The things that were taken at the Light house were vendued and went very high[172] Nothing more remarkable hapned
this day at night their was a regular deserted from the enimy.

the 21. I went upon the creek guard[173] and it rained all day
nothing remarkable hapned.

the 22. Being Sunday nothing remarkable this day.

the 23. Nothing remarkable hapned at night I went upon the piquet and nothing hapned worth a mentioning.

the 24. Nothing remarkable hapned this day onely we heard that
the french were a going to join us upon conditions that we would
trade with them.[174]

the 25. We turned out and went to the Larm post and (p. 079) it
was very cold and we came home and there was a high go of Drink-
ing Brandy and several of the company were taken not well prety
soon after[175] nothing more this day.

the 26. This morning early their was several Laidies came down
from wrentham and they went to cambridg and the rest of their acts
are they not writen in the Lamentations of Samuel Haws, finis.

the 27. This day I went upon fatigue and we got our Stents done
about noon.

the 28. Nothing remarkable this day onely I was chose cook for
our room consisting of 12 men and a hard game too.

the 29. Being Sunday the officers had hard work to get hands for
meting it was so cold nothing more this day.

the 30. This day nothing remarkable hapned.

the 31. Nothing remarkable.[176]

November 1775.

the 1. Las night the fire ran over Samuel Hawes's hair and that
provoket him to wrath Nothing very remarkable hapned this day
that I know of.

the 2. their was Some gentlemen and Laidies came down from
Wrentham and they went to cambridg.

the (p. 080) 3. It was a very rainy day and we went to childses and had an old fudg fairyouwell my friends.

the 4. Nothing remarkable hapned this day onely the gentry went home to Wrentham.

the 5. Being the memorial 5th of novem. the enemy fired from every Ship in the harbour nothing more remarkable this day.

the 6. Nothing remarkable hapned this day.

the 7. Their was a vendue opened att this house and their was not Less than a hundred and twenty Dollars worth of things vendued and sold at private sale and Swapt.

the 8. Nothing remarkable hapned this day that I know of.

the 9. Nothing remarkable hapned this day that is worth amentioning.[177]

the 10. This day I went home upon furlow,[178] yesterday Sergent Yett went home.

the 11. I went to captain whitings and nothing remarkable hapned.

the 12. Being Sunday I went to meting Nothing more this day.

the 13. This day the Long faced People trained at Wrentham and Serg Felt went upon the piquet and fired several times upon the centrys.

the 14. This day I came down from Wrentham with Serg (p. 081) Felt and at night their was three men deserted from the floating Battery this day we had a Lottery and Serg Foster drawd a pair of Breeches[179] worth 5 Dollars and their was considerable other tradeing caried on at night their was 8 men more deserted.

the 16. Nothing remarkable hapned captain Pond Listed three or four men for the next campaign[180] att night it was very cold.

the 17. Very blustering and their was a man Whipt thirty and nine Lashes for Stealing and getting Drunk and running away and afterwards he was drummed out of the camps thus he &c.

the 18. Nothing remarkable hapned this day that I know of.

the 19. This day being Sunday it was very pleasant and we had Preaching Nothing more this day.

the 20. This day nothing very remarkable at night their was a regular deserted and Swam over to Dorchester and escaped.

the (p. 082) 21. This day Nothing very remarkable this day the piquet was made easier by half &c. &c.

the 22. To morrow is thanksgiveing this day ended without any thing remarkable.

the 23. Being thanksgiveing I went with Serg Felt up to newtown and kept thanksgiveing their and returnd to our Barricks at night and we had not ben a bed long when our captain came to us and ordered us all to Lye upon our arms by order of General Washington Lesemo[181] of the American Army incampt at cambridg and roxbury and other places[182] nothing more this day that I know of onely 2 regulars deserted at night on cambridg side.[183]

the 24. Nothing hapned very remarkable this day that I know of.

the 25. This morning Captain Pond inlisted several men for the next campaign; o you nasty Sloven how your Book Looks.[184]

the 26. Being Sunday it was Stormy Nothing remarkable this day.

the (p. 083) 27. Nothing very remarkable hapned this day.

the 28. Nothing very Strange onely Peperiss curacle came out of Boston that old tory Dog.

the 29. Nothing remarkable onely one of our Privateers took a prize richly Laden.[185]

the 30. Nothing extreordenary this day that I know of.

December.

the 1. Nothing remarkable this day.

the 2. This day I with a number of rispectable gentlemen went[186]....

the (p. 084) 3. Being Sunday it rained nothing remarkable hapned this day.

the 4. Nothing remarkable hapnd this day at night we were ordered to Ly upon our arms.[187]

the 5. Nothing Strange hapned this day.

the 6. Nothing comical this day only their was considerable of tradeing caryd on.[188]

the 7. This day nothing Strang.

the 8. This day I with several more inlisted for the year 1776 under captain Oliver Pond.

the 9. Nothing remarkable this day.

the 10. This day the Long faced People[189] arived here from wrentham and other places.

the 11. This day I past muster before general Spencer[190] nothing more this day.

the 12. This day it was very cold and the melitia had to mount guard that is good for them.

the 13. This day I went to cambridg and viewed the works on copple[191] hill.[192]

the (p. 085) 14. This day I went to Watertown[193] with Lieutenant Bacon and a number of others in order to get some coats but we could not find any that suited us and so we returned.[194]

the 15. This day nothing very remarkable.

the 16. This day nothing strange at night their was an atempt made to blow up A Ship but it failed also this night we heard that Quebeck was taken.[195]

the 17. Being Sunday it was foul weather nothing remarkable hapned this day onely the enemy fired at our men on Lechmers[196] Point and wounded one and our men returned the fire from copple hill.

the 18. This day the Ship moved out of the Bay and the Enemy threw Bombs from mount Hoordom[197] but did no Damage.

the 19. This day nothing remarkable hapned.

the 20. Nothing strange this day.

the 21. This day it was very cold nothing strange this day.

the 22. Nothing remarkable this day.

the (p. 086) 23. Nothing strange this day.

the 24. Ditto Ditto Ditto.

the 25. Good.

the 26. Very cold this day nothing remarkable this day.

the 27. Nothing remarkable to day.

the 28. Nothing strange this day.

the 29. Nothing strange this day Last Night our men made an atempt to take Bunker hill but their Scheem was frustrated &c.[198]

the 30, 31. Nothing remarkable.

January.

the 1. A Happy new year 1776 Behold the man three score and ten upon a Dying Bed he'se run his race and get no Grace and Awful Sight indeed Nothing very remarkable this 1 day of January 1776 Anoquedomina.[199]

the 2. Nothing strange this day.

the 3. 20 men out of each Regement in Roxbury side to cut fachines[200] I believe we have it by and by.

the (p. 087) 4. Nothing remarkable this day.

the 5-7. Nothing strange.

the 8. At night some of our brave heroick Americans went Past the Enemys Brest Work at Bunker hill and burnt several housen at the foot of Bunker hill and took 5 men and 1 woman Prisoners and came of as far as copple hill when the flames began to extend and the enemy that were in the fort perceiving a number of men gather round the fire & suposing them to be our men they kept up a bright fire for the space of near half an hour upon their own men devil-lightfooly[201] they[202]....

the 9. Nothing remarkable this day.

the 10. Nothing very remarkable this day it was very cold.

the 11. Nothing very remarkable this day.

the 12. All furlows stopt this day.

the (p. 088) 13. Nothing strange this day.

the 14. Being Sunday nothing remarkable this day.

the 15. This day we heard that the regulars had taken Providence and burnt all the housen except two.[203]

the 16. Nothing remarkable hapened this day at night we were all ordered to Ly upon our arms.

the 17. This day we had the disagreeable news that our men were defeated that went to Quebeck and that General montgomery and colonel Arnold were either killed or taken Prisoners but we Pray God thy news may prove falce[204] at night it was thought their was a spy out from Boston and our centrys fired at him but we dont know the Sertainty of it cold weather for the Season.

the 18. Nothing strange this day.

the (p. 089) 19. This day we heard that our men had taken a Ship Loaded with Gunpowder the truth of it we have not yet Learned but we hope it will prove true.[205]

the 20. Nothing remarkable this day.

the 21. Ditto.

the 22. Nothing strange.

the 23. Nothing remarkable.

the 24. This day capt Pond came from Wrentham Nothing re-markable.

the 25. Nothing remarkable this day.

the 26. Nothing very remarkable.

the 27. Nothing remarkable this day.

the 28. Nothing remarkable.

the 29. This day we moved to Dorchester into the widow Birds house.

the 30. Nothing strange this day.

the 31. Ditto.

February.

the 1. This day nothing remarkable.

the 2. Ditto.

the 3. Nothing Remarkable this day.

the 4. Ditto.

the 5. The Lobsters came out almost to copple hill and took 3 cows and killed them and were fired upon from (p. 090) copple hill and they were obligd to mak of Leaving their Booty behind them.

the 6. The melitious men[206] marched from Wrentham and arived in camp at Dorchester.

the 7. Nothing very remarkable this day.

the 8. Their was a number of our men went a Scating on the Bay near Bosston common and the Enemy fired upwards of a hundred small arms that did no damage.

the 9. Nothing very remarkable at night their was thre of our Amarican Boys made their escape from the Enemy in Boston and were taken up by our men who were Patroling on Dorchester Point to and they brought of things to considerable value.

the 10. Nothing Strange this day.[207]

SUPPLEMENT,
(p. 091) CONTAINING
OFFICIAL PAPERS ON THE SKIRMISHES AT LEXINGTON AND CONCORD,
AND A LIST OF REVOLUTIONARY ARTICLES IN THE POUGHKEEPSIE MUSEUM.

SUPPLEMENT.

(p. 093)

OFFICIAL PAPERS
concerning
THE SKIRMISHES AT LEXINGTON AND CONCORD.

In the preceding Journal of a Soldier, in 1775, his narrative commences on the day of the skirmishes at Lexington and Concord, the opening conflicts of the Revolution. Some official matters relating to those events, which are inaccessible to the general reading-public, will doubtless be acceptable, as they certainly are appropriate, in this connection.

The skirmishes occurred on the 19th of April, 1775. On the 22d, the Provincial Congress of Massachusetts assembled, and, deeming it important to have the whole truth known, appointed a committee to take depositions in relation to the transactions of the British troops in their route to and from Concord. Another committee was appointed the following day, consisting of Dr. Church, Elbridge Gerry, and Thomas Cushing, to draw up a narrative of the massacre. The committee to take (p. 094) depositions held their sessions at Concord and Lexington, on the 23d and 25th of April. Feeling it to be expedient to send an account immediately to England, a committee, consisting of Dr. Warren, Mr. Freeman, Mr. Gardiner, and Colonel Stone, was chosen to prepare a letter to Dr. Franklin, the colonial agent in London. They reported a letter, and also an "Address to the Inhabitants of Great Britain," on the same day. Captain Richard Derby, of Salem, was employed to proceed immediately with the despatches. He placed them in the hands of Doctor Franklin on the 29th of May, and on the following day the address was printed and circulated. It gave the first intelligence of the skirmishes at Lexington and Concord, to the British public.

The following, copied from the Journals of the Continental Congress, are the several papers referred to: —

"To the Hon. Benjamin Franklin, Esq., at London.

"In Provincial Congress, Watertown, *April 26, 1775.*

"Sir: From the entire confidence we repose in your faithfulness and abilities, we consider it the happiness of this colony that the important trust of agency for it, in this day of unequalled distress, is devolved on your hands, and we doubt not your attachment to the cause and liberties of mankind will make every possible exertion in our behalf a pleasure to you; although our circumstances will compel us often to interrupt your (p. 095) repose, by matters that will surely give you pain. A singular instance hereof is the occasion of the present letter. The contents of this packet will be our apology for troubling you with it.

"From these you will see how, and by whom, we are at last plunged into the horrors of a most unnatural war.

"Our enemies, we are told, have despatched to Great Britain a fallacious account of the tragedy they have begun; to prevent the operation of which to the public injury, we have engaged the vessel that conveys this to you, as a packet in the service of this colony, and we request your assistance in supplying Captain Derby, who commands her, with such necessaries as he shall want, on the credit of your constituents in Massachusetts Bay.

"But we most ardently wish that the several papers herewith enclosed may be immediately printed and dispersed through every town in England, and especially communicated to the lord-mayor, aldermen, and council, of the city of London, that they may take such order thereon as they may think proper. And we are confident your fidelity will make such improvement of them as shall convince all, who are not determined to be in everlasting blindness, that it is the united efforts of both Englands that can save either: but that whatever price our brethren in the one may be pleased to put on their constitutional liberties, we are authorized to assure you that the inhabitants of the other, with the greatest (p. 096) unanimity, are inflexibly resolved to sell theirs only at the price of their lives.

"Signed by order of the Provincial Congress,
"Joseph Warren, *President, P. T.*
"A true copy from the original minutes,
"Samuel Freeman, *Sec. P. T.*"

The depositions relative to the commencement of hostilities are as follows:—

"Lexington, *April 25, 1775.*

"We, Solomon Brown, Jonathan Loring, and Elijah Sanderson, all of lawful age, and of Lexington, in the county of Middlesex, and colony of the Massachusetts Bay in New England, do testify and declare that, on the evening of the 18th of April, instant, being on the road between Concord and Lexington, and all of us mounted on horses, we were, about ten of the clock, suddenly surprised by nine persons, whom we took to be regular officers, who rode up to us, mounted and armed, each having a pistol in his hand, and, after putting pistols to our breasts, and seizing the bridles of our horses, they swore, if we stirred another step, we should be all dead men, upon which we surrendered ourselves. They detained us until two o'clock the next morning, in which time they searched and greatly abused us, having first inquired about the magazine at Concord, whether any guards were posted there, and whether the bridges were up, and said four or five regiments of regulars would be in possession of the stores soon. They then brought us back to Lexington, cut the (p. 097) horses' bridles and girths, turned them loose, and then left us.

"Solomon Brown,
"Jonathan Loring, Elijah Sanderson."

   "Lexington, *April 25, 1775*.

   "I, Elijah Sanderson, above named, do further testify and declare, that I was on Lexington common, the morning of the 19th of April aforesaid, having been dismissed by the officers above mentioned, and saw a large body of regular troops advancing toward Lexington company, many of whom were then dispersing. I heard one of the regulars, whom I took to be an officer, say, "Damn them, we will have them;" and immediately the regulars shouted aloud, run and fired upon the Lexington company, which did not fire a gun before the regulars discharged on them. Eight of the Lexington company were killed while they were dispersing, and at a considerable distance from each other, and many wounded; and, although a spectator, I narrowly escaped with my life.

   "Elijah Sanderson."

   "Lexington, *April 23, 1775*.

   "I, Thomas Rice Willard, of lawful age, do testify and declare that, being in the house of Daniel Harrington, of said Lexington, on the 19th instant, in the morning, about half an hour before sunrise, looked out at the window of said house, and saw (as I suppose) about four hundred regulars in one body, coming up the road, and marched toward the north part of the common, back (p. 098) of the meeting-house of said Lexington; and as soon as said regulars were against the east end of the meeting-house, the commanding officer said something, what I know not, but upon that the regulars ran till they came within about eight or nine rods of about a hundred of the militia of Lexington, who were collected on said common, at which time the militia of Lexington dispersed. Then the officers made a huzza, and the private soldiers succeeded them: directly after this, an officer rode before the regulars to the other side of the body, and hallooed after the militia of said Lexington, and said, "Lay down your arms, damn you, why don't you lay down your arms?"—and that there was not a gun fired till the militia of Lexington were dispersed. And further saith not.

"Thomas Rice Willard."

"Lexington, *April 25, 1775.*

"Simon Winship, of Lexington, in the county of Middlesex, and province of Massachusetts Bay, New England, being of lawful age, testifieth and saith, that on the 19th April instant, about four o'clock in the morning, as he was passing the public road in said Lexington, peaceably and unarmed, about two miles and a half distant from the meeting-house in said Lexington, he was met by a body of the king's regular troops, and being stopped by some officers of said troops, was commanded to dismount. Upon asking why he must dismount, he was obliged by force to quit his horse, and ordered (p. 099) to march in the midst of the body; and, being examined whether he had been warning the minute-men, he answered, 'No, but had been out, and was then returning to his father's.' Said Winship farther testifies that he marched with said troops, till he came within about half a quarter of a mile of said meeting-house, where an officer commanded the troops to halt, and then to prime and load: this being done, the said troops marched on till they came within a few rods of Captain Parker's company, who were partly collected on the place of parade, when said Winship observed an officer at the head of said troops, flourishing his sword, and with a loud voice giving the word, 'Fire! fire!' which was instantly followed by a discharge of arms from said regular troops; and said Winship is positive, and in the most solemn manner declares, that there was no discharge of arms on either side, till the word 'Fire' was given by the said officer as above.

"Simon Winship."

Lexington, *April 25, 1775.*

"I, John Parker, of lawful age, and commander of the militia in Lexington, do testify and declare that, on the 19th instant, in the morning, about one of the clock, being informed that there were a number of regula-officers riding up and down the road, stopping and insulting people as they passed the road; and also was informed that a number of regular troops were on their march from Boston, in order to take the province stores at (p. 100) Concord, ordered our militia to meet on the common in said Lexington, to consult what to do, and concluded not to be discovered, nor meddle or make with said regular troops (if they should approach), unless they should insult or molest us; and, upon their sudden approach, I immediately ordered our militia to disperse, and not to fire. Immediately said troops made their appearance, and rushed furiously, fired upon, and killed eight of our party, without receiving any provocation therefor from us.

"John Parker."

Lexington, *April 24, 1775.*

"I, John Robins, being of lawful age, do testify and say that, on the 19th instant, the company under the command of Captain John Parker, being drawn up (some time before sunrise) on the green or common, and I being in the front rank, there suddenly appeared a number of the king's troops, about a thousand, as I thought, at the distance of about sixty or seventy yards from us, huzzaing, and on a quick pace toward us, with three officers in their front on horseback, and on full gallop toward us, the foremost of which cried, 'Throw down your arms, ye villains, ye rebels!' upon which said company dispersing, the foremost of the three officers ordered their men, saying, 'Fire, by God! fire!' at which moment we received a very heavy and close fire from them; at which instant, being wounded, I fell, and several of our men were shot dead by me. Captain (p. 101)

Parker's men, I believe, had not then fired a gun. And further the deponent saith not.

"John Robins."

"Lexington, *April 25, 1775.*

"We, Benjamin Tidd, of Lexington, and Joseph Abbot, of Lincoln, in the county of Middlesex, and colony of Massachusetts Bay, in New England, of lawful age, do testify and declare that, on the morning of the 19th of April instant, about five o'clock, being on Lexington common, and mounted on horses, we saw a body of regular troops marching up to the Lexington company, which was then dispersing. Soon after, the regulars fired, first, a few guns, which we took to be pistols from some of the regulars who were mounted on horses, and then the said regulars fired a volley or two before any guns were fired by the Lexington company; our horses immediately started, and we rode off. And further say not.

"Benjamin Tidd, Joseph Abbot."

"Lexington, *April 25, 1775.*

"We, Nathaniel Mullokin, Philip Russell, Moses Harrington, jun., Thomas and Daniel Harrington, William Grimes, William Tidd, Isaac Hastings, Jonas Stone, jun., James Wyman, Thaddeus Harrington, John Chandler, Joshua Reed, jun., Joseph Simonds, Phineas Smith, John Chandler, jun., Reuben Cock, Joel Viles, Nathan Reed, Samuel Tidd, Benjamin Lock, Thomas Winship, (p. 102) Simeon Snow, John Smith, Moses Harrington the 3d, Joshua Reed, Ebenezer Parker, John Harrington, Enoch Willington, John Hornier, Isaac Green, Phineas Stearns, Isaac Durant, and Thomas Headley, jun., all of lawful age, and inhabitants of Lexington, in the county of Middlesex, and colony of the Massachusetts Bay, in New England, do testify and declare, that, on the 19th of April instant, about one or two o'clock in the morning, being informed that several officers of the regulars had, the evening before, been riding up and down the road, and had detained and insulted the inhabitants passing the same; and also understanding that a body of regulars were marching from Boston toward Concord, with intent (as it was supposed) to take the stores, belonging to the colony, in that town, we were alarmed, and having met at the place of our company's parade, were dismissed by our captain, John Parker, for the present, with orders to be ready to attend at the beat of the drum. We further testify and declare, that, about five o'clock in the morning, hearing our drum beat, we proceeded toward the parade, and soon found that a large body of troops were marching toward us. Some of our company were coming up to the parade, and others had reached it, at which time the company began to disperse. While our backs were turned on the troops, we were fired on by them, and a number of our men were instantly killed and wounded. Not a gun was fired by any person in our company on the regulars, to our knowledge, before they (p. 103) fired on us, and they continued firing until we had all made our escape.

"Signed by each of the above deponents,"

"Lexington, *25th of April, 1775.*

"We, Nathaniel Parkhurst, Jonas Parker, John Munroe, jun., John Winship, Solomon Pierce, John Muzzy, Abner Meeds, John Bridge, jun., Ebenezer Bowman, William Munroe the 3d, Micah Hager, Samuel Saunderson, Samuel Hastings, and James Brown, of Lexington, in the county of Middlesex, and colony of the Massachusetts Bay, in New England, and all of lawful age, do testify and say, that, on the morning of the 19th of April instant, about one or two o'clock, being informed that a number of regular officers had been riding up and down the road the evening and night preceding, and that some of the inhabitants, as they were passing, had been insulted by the officers, and stopped by them; and being also informed that the regular troops were on their march from Boston, in order (as it was said) to take the colony stores then deposited at Concord, we met on the parade of our company in this town. After the company had collected, we were ordered by Captain Parker (who commanded us) to disperse for the present, and to be ready to attend the beat of the drum; and accordingly the company went into houses near the place of parade. We further testify and say, that, about five o'clock in the morning, we attended the beat of our drum, and were formed (p. 104) on the parade; we were faced toward the regulars then marching up to us, and some of our company were coming to the parade with their backs toward the troops, and others, on the parade, began to disperse, when the regulars fired on the company, before a gun was fired by any of our company on them. They killed eight of our company, and wounded several, and continued their fire until we had all made our escape.

"Signed by each of the deponents."

"Lexington, *April 25, 1775.*

"I, Timothy Smith, of Lexington, in the county of Middlesex, and colony of Massachusetts Bay, in New England, being of lawful age, do testify and declare, that, on the morning of the 19th of April instant, being on Lexington common, as a spectator, I saw a large body of regular troops marching up toward the Lexington company, then dispersing, and likewise saw the regular troops fire on the Lexington company, before the latter fired a gun. I immediately ran, and a volley was discharged at me, which put me in imminent danger of losing my life. I soon returned to the common, and saw eight of the Lexington men who were killed, and lay bleeding at a considerable distance from each other; and several were wounded. And further saith not.

"Timothy Smith."

"Lexington, *April 25, 1775.*

"We, Levi Mead and Levi Harrington, both of Lexington, in the county of Middlesex, and colony of Massachusetts Bay, (p. 105) in New England, and of lawful age, do testify and declare, that, on the morning of the 19th of April, being on Lexington commons, as spectators, we saw a large body of regular troops marching up toward the Lexington company; and some of the regulars, on horses, whom we took to be officers, fired a pistol or two on the Lexington company, which was then dispersing. These were the first guns that were fired, and they were immediately followed by several volleys from the regulars, by which eight men belonging to said company were killed, and several wounded.

"Levi Harrington, Levi Mead."

"Lexington, *April 25, 1775.*

"I, William Draper, of lawful age, and an inhabitant of Colrain, in the county of Hampshire, and colony of Massachusetts Bay, in New England, do testify and declare, that, being on the parade of said

Lexington, April 19th instant, about half an hour before sunrise, the king's regular troops appeared at the meeting-house of Lexington. Captain Parker's company, who were drawn up back of said meeting-house on the parade, turned from said troops, making their escape, by dispersing. In the meantime, the regular troops made a huzza, and ran toward Captain Parker's company, who were dispersing; and, immediately after the huzza was made, the commanding officer of said troops (as I took him) gave the command to the said troops — "Fire! fire! damn you, fire!" — and immediately they fired, before (p. 106) any of Captain Parker's company fired, I then being within three or four rods of said regular troops. And further say not.

"William Draper."

"Lexington, *April 23, 1775.*

"I, Thomas Fessenden, of lawful age, testify and declare, that, being in a pasture near the meeting-house, at said Lexington, on Wednesday last, at about half an hour before sunrise, I saw a number of regular troops pass speedily by said meeting-house, on their way toward a company of militia of said Lexington, who were assembled to the number of about one hundred in a company, at the distance of eighteen or twenty rods from said meeting-house; and after they had passed by said meeting-house, I saw three officers, on horseback, advance to the front of said regulars, when one of them, being within six rods of the said militia, cried out, "Disperse, you rebels, immediately!" on which he brandished his sword over his head three times: meanwhile, the second officer, who was about two rods behind him, fired a pistol, pointed at said militia, and the regulars kept huzzaing till he had finished brandishing his sword; and when he had thus finished brandishing his sword, he pointed it down toward said militia, and immediately on which the said regulars fired a volley at the militia, and then I ran off as fast as I could, while they continued firing till I got out of their reach. I further testify, that, as soon as ever the officer cried, "Disperse, you rebels," the said company of militia dispersed (p. 107) every way, as fast as they could; and, while they were dispersing, the regulars kept firing at them incessantly. And further saith not.

"Thomas Fessenden."

"Lincoln, *April 23, 1775.*

"I, John Bateman, belonging to the fifty-second regiment, commanded by Colonel Jones, on Wednesday morning, on the 19th day of April instant, was in the party marching to Concord, being at Lexington, in the county of Middlesex, being nigh the meeting-house in said Lexington, there was a small party of men gathered together at that place, when our said troops marched by; and I testify and declare that I heard the word of command given to the troops to fire, and some of said troops did fire, and I saw one of said small party lay dead on the ground nigh said meeting-house; and I testify that I never heard any of the inhabitants so much as fire one gun on said troops.

"John Bateman."

"Lexington, *April 23, 1775.*

"We, John Hoar, John Whithead, Abraham Garfield, Benjamin Munroe, Isaac Parks, William Hosmer, John Adams, Gregory Stone, all of Lincoln, in the county of Middlesex, Massachusetts Bay, all of lawful age, do testify and say that, on Wednesday last, we were assembled at Concord, in the morning of said day, in consequence of information received that a brigade of regular troops were on their march to the said town of (p. 108) Concord, who had killed six men at the town of Lexington. About an hour afterward, we saw them approaching, to the number, as we apprehended, of about twelve hundred, on which we retreated to a hill about eighty rods back, and the said troops then took possession of the hill where we were first posted. Presently after this we saw the troops moving toward the north bridge, about one mile from the said Concord meeting-house. We then immediately went before them and passed the bridge just before a party of them, to the number of about two hundred, arrived. They there left about one half of their two hundred at the bridge, and proceeded with the rest toward Colonel Barrett's, about two miles from the said bridge. We then, seeing several fires in the town, thought the houses in Concord were in danger, and marched toward the said bridge; and the troops that were stationed there, observing our approach, marched back over the bridge, and then took up some of the planks. We then hastened our march toward the bridge, and, when we had got near the bridge, they fired on our men—first three guns, one after the other, and then a considerable number more; and then, and not before (having orders from our commanding officers not to fire till we were fired upon), we fired upon the regulars, and they retreated. On their retreat through the town of Lexington to Charlestown, they ravaged and destroyed private property, and burnt three houses, one barn, and one shop.

"Signed by each of the above deponents."

"Lexington, *April 23, 1775.* (p. 109)

"We, Nathan Barret, captain; Jonathan Farrar, Joseph Butler, and Francis Wheeler, lieutenants; John Barret, ensign; John Brown, Silas Walker, Ephraim Melvin, Nathan Buttrick, Stephen Hosmer, jun., Samuel Barret, Thomas Jones, Joseph Chandler, Peter Wheeler, Nathan Pierce, and Edward Richardson, all of Concord, in the county of Middlesex, in the province of Massachusetts Bay, of lawful age, testify and declare, that, on Wednesday, the 19th instant, about an hour after sunrise, we assembled on a hill near the meeting-house in Concord aforesaid, in consequence of an information that a number of regular troops had killed six of our countrymen at Lexington, and were on their march to said Concord; and, about an hour afterward, we saw them approaching, to the number, as we imagine, of about twelve hundred; on which we retreated to a hill about eighty rods back, and the aforesaid troops then took possession of a hill where we were first posted. Presently after this, we saw them moving toward the north bridge, about one mile from said meeting-house; we then immediately went before them, and passed the bridge just before a party of them, to the number of about two hundred, arrived. They there left about one half of these two hundred at the bridge, and proceeded with the rest toward Colonel Barret's, about two miles from the said bridge. We then, seeing several fires in the town thought our houses were in danger, and immediately marched back toward said bridge, and (p. 110) the troops who were stationed there, observing our approach, marched back over the bridge, and then took up some of the planks. We then hastened our steps toward the bridge, and when we had got near the bridge, they fired on our men—first three guns, one after the other, and then a considerable number more; upon which, and not before (having orders from our commanding officer not to fire till we were fired upon), we fired upon the regulars, and they retreated. At Concord, and on their retreat through Lexington, they plundered many houses, burnt three at Lexington, together with a shop and barn, and committed damage, more or less, to almost every house from Concord to Charlestown.

"Signed by the above deponents."

"We, Joseph Butler and Ephraim Melvin, do testify and declare, that, when the regular troops fired upon our people at the north bridge, in Concord, as related in the foregoing depositions, they shot one, and we believe two, of our people, before we fired a single gun at them.

"Joseph Butler, Ephraim Melvin.
"Lexington, *April 23, 1775.*"

"Concord, *April 23, 1775.*

"I, Timothy Minot, jun., of Concord, on the 19th day of this instant, April, after that I had heard of the regular troops firing upon Lexington men, and fearing that hostilities might be committed at Concord, thought it my incumbent duty to secure my family. After I had secured (p. 111) my family, some time after that, returning toward my own dwelling, and finding that the bridge on the north part of said Concord was guarded by regular troops, being a spectator of what had happened at said bridge, declare that the regular troops stationed on said bridge, after they saw the men that were collected on the westerly side of said bridge, marched toward said bridge; then the troops returned toward the easterly side of said bridge, and formed themselves, as I thought, for regular fight: after that they fired one gun, then two or three more, before the men that were stationed on the westerly part of said bridge fired upon them.

"Timothy Minot, jun."

"Lexington, *April 23, 1775.*

"I, James Barret, of Concord, colonel of a regiment of militia, in the county of Middlesex, do testify and say that, on Wednesday morning last, about daybreak, I was informed of the approach of a number of the regular troops to the town of Concord, where were some magazines belonging to this province, when there was assembled some of the militia of this and the neighboring towns, I ordered them to march to the north bridge (so called), which they had passed and were taking up. I ordered said militia to march to said bridge and pass the same, but not to fire on the king's troops unless they were first fired upon. We advanced near said bridge, when the said troops fired upon our militia, and killed two men dead on the spot, and wounded (p. 112) several others, which was the first firing of guns in the town of Concord. My detachment then returned the fire, which killed and wounded several of the king's troops.

"James Barret."

"Lexington, *April 23, 1775.*

"We, Bradbury Robinson, Samuel Spring, Thaddeus Bancroft, all of Concord, and James Adams, of Lexington, all in the county of Middlesex, all of lawful age, do testify and say, that, on Wednesday morning last, near ten of the clock, we saw near one hundred of the regular troops, being in the town of Concord, at the north bridge in said town (so called); and having passed the same, they were taking up said bridge, when about three hundred of our militia were advancing toward said bridge, in order to pass said bridge, when, without saying anything to us, they discharged a number of guns on us, which killed two men dead on the spot, and wounded several others; when we returned the fire on them, which killed two of them, and wounded several, which was the beginning of hostilities in the town of Concord.

"Bradbury Robinson, Thaddeus Bancroft,
"Samuel Spring, James Adams."

"Worcester, *April 26, 1775.*

"Hannah Bradish, of that part of Cambridge called Menotomy, and daughter of Timothy Paine, of Worcester, in the county of Worcester, Esq., of lawful age, testifies (p. 113) and says, that, about five o'clock on Wednesday last, afternoon, being in her bedchamber, with her infant child, about eight days old, she was surprised by the firing of the king's troops and our people, on their return from Concord. She being weak and unable to go out of her house, in order to secure herself and family, they all retired into the kitchen, in the back part of the house. She soon found the house surrounded with the king's troops; that upon observation made, at least seventy bullets were shot into the front part of the house; several bullets lodged in the kitchen where she was, and one passed through an easy-chair she had just gone from. The door of the front part of the house was broke open; she did not see any soldiers in the house, but supposed, by the noise, they were in the front. After the troops had gone off, she missed the following things, which, she verily believes, were taken out of the house by the king's troops, viz., one rich brocade gown, called a negligee, one lutestring gown, one white quilt, one pair of brocade shoes, three shifts, eight white aprons, three caps, one case of ivory knives and forks, and several other small articles.

"Hannah Bradish."

Province of the Massachusetts Bay,Worcester, ss., *April 26, 1775.*

"Mrs. Hannah Bradish, the above deponent, maketh oath before us, the subscribers, two of his majesty's justices of the peace for the county of Worcester, and of the quorum, that the above deposition, according to her (p. 114) best recollection, is the truth. Which deposition is taken in *perpetuam rei memoriam.*

"Thomas Steel,
"Timothy Paine."

"Concord, *April 23, 1775.*

"I, James Marr, of lawful age, testify and say, that, in the evening of the 18th instant, I received orders from George Hutchinson, adjutant of the fourth regiment of the regular troops stationed at Boston, to prepare and march: to which orders I attended, and marched to Concord, where I was ordered by an officer with about one hundred men to guard a certain bridge there. While attending that service, a number of people came along, in order, as I suppose, to cross said bridge, at which time a number of the regular troops first fired upon them.

"James Marr."

"Medford, *April 25, 1775.*

"I, Edward Thoroton Gould, of his majesty's own regiment of foot, being of lawful age, do testify and declare, that, on the evening of the 18th instant, under the orders of General Gage, I embarked with the light infantry and grenadiers of the line, commanded by Colonel Smith, and landed on the marshes of Cambridge, from whence we proceeded to Lexington. On our arrival at that place, we saw a body of provincial troops, armed, to the number of about sixty or seventy men. On our approach, they dispersed, and soon after firing (p. 115) began, but which party fired first I can not exactly say, as our troops rushed on shouting and huzzaing previous to the firing, which was continued by our troops so long as any of the provincials were to be seen. From thence we marched to Concord. On a hill, near the entrance of the town, we saw another body of provincials assembled: the light-infantry companies were ordered up the hill to disperse them; on our approach, they retreated toward Concord. The grenadiers continued the road under the hill toward the town. Six companies of light infantry were ordered down to take possession of the bridge which the provincials retreated over; the company I commanded was one. Three companies of the above detachment went forward about two miles. In the meantime, the provincial troops returned, to the number of about three or four hundred. We drew up on the Concord side of the bridge; the provincials came down upon us, upon which we engaged and gave the first fire. This was the first engagement after the one at Lexington. A continued firing from both parties lasted through the whole day. I myself was wounded at the attack of the bridge, and am now treated with the greatest humanity, and taken all possible care of by the provincials at Medford.

"Edward Thoroton Gould,
"*Lieut. King's Own Regiment.*"
"Province of Massachusetts Bay,
"*Middlesex County, April 25, 1775.*

"Lieutenant Thoroton Gould, aforenamed, personally made (p. 116) oath to the truth of the foregoing declaration by him subscribed, before us,

"Thad. Masson,
"Josiah Johnson, Simon Tufts, *Justices of the peace for the county aforesaid, quorum unus.*"

"Province of Massachusetts Bay, Charlestown, ss.

"I, Nathaniel Gorham, notary and tabellion public, by lawful authority duly admitted and sworn, hereby certify to all whom it may or doth concern, that Thaddeus Masson, Josiah Johnson, and Simon Tufts, Esqrs., are three of his majesty's justices of the peace (*quorum unus*) for the county of Middlesex; and that full faith and credit is and ought to be given to their transactions as such, both in court and out. In witness whereof, I have hereunto affixed my name and seal, this twenty-sixth day of April, *Anno Domini* one thousand seven hundred and seventy-five.

"Nathaniel Gorham, *Notary Public*." (L. S.)

(All the above depositions are sworn to before justices of the peace, and duly attested by notaries public, in manner of the last one.)

"In Provincial Congress, Watertown, *April 26, 1775.*
"*To the Inhabitants of Great Britain.*

"Friends and Fellow-Subjects: Hostilities are at length commenced in this colony by the troops under the command of General Gage; and it being of the greatest importance that an early, true, and authentic account (p. 117) of this inhuman proceeding, should be known to you, the Congress of this colony have transmitted the same, and, from want of a session of the Hon. Continental Congress, think it proper to address you on the alarming occasion.

"By the clearest depositions relative to this transaction, it will appear that, on the night preceding the 19th of April instant, a body of the king's troops, under the command of Colonel Smith, were secretly landed at Cambridge, with an apparent design to take or destroy the military and other stores, provided for the defence of this colony, and deposited at Concord; that some inhabitants of the colony, on the night aforesaid, while travelling peaceably on the road between Boston and Concord, were seized and greatly abused by armed men, who appeared to be officers of General Gage's army; that the town of Lexington by these means was alarmed, and a company of the inhabitants mustered on the occasion; that the regular troops, on their way to Concord, marched into the said town of Lexington, and the said company on their approach began to disperse; that notwithstanding this, the regulars rushed on with great violence, and first began hostilities, by firing on said Lexington company, whereby they killed eight, and wounded several others; that the regulars continued their fire until those of said company, who were neither killed nor wounded, had made their escape; that Colonel Smith, with the detachment, then marched to Concord, where a number of provincials were again fired (p. 118) on by the troops, two of them killed and several wounded, before the provincials fired on them; and that these hostile measures of the troops produced an engagement that lasted through the day, in which many of the provincials and more of the regular troops were killed and wounded.

"To give a particular account of the ravages of the troops, as they retreated from Concord to Charlestown, would be very difficult, if not impracticable. Let it suffice to say, that a great number of the houses on the road were plundered, and rendered unfit for use; several were burnt; women in childbed were driven, by the soldiery, naked into the streets; old men peaceably in their houses were shot dead; and such scenes exhibited as would disgrace the annals of the most uncivilized nations.

"These, brethren, are marks of ministerial vengeance against this colony, for refusing, with her sister-colonies, a submission to slavery; but they have not yet detached us from our royal sovereign. We profess to be his loyal and dutiful subjects, and so hardly dealt with as we have been, are still ready, with our lives and fortunes, to defend his person, family, crown, and dignity. Nevertheless, to the persecution and tyranny of his cruel ministry we will not tamely submit: appealing to Heaven for the justice of our cause, we determine to die or be free.

"We can not think that the honor, wisdom, and valor of Britons will suffer them to be long inactive spectators of (p. 119) measures in which they themselves are so deeply interested—measures pursued in opposition to the solemn protests of many noble lords, and expressed sense of conspicuous commoners, whose knowledge and virtue have long characterized them as some of the greatest men in the nation—measures executing contrary to the interest, petitions, and resolves of many large, respectable, and opulent counties, cities, and boroughs in Great Britain—measures highly incompatible with justice, but still pursued with a specious pretence of easing the nation of its burdens—measures which, if successful, must end in the ruin and slavery of Britain, as well as the persecuted American colonies.

"We sincerely hope that the great Sovereign of the universe, who hath so often appeared for the English nation, will support you in every rational and manly exertion, with these colonies, for saving it from ruin; and that, in a constitutional connection with the mother-country, we shall soon be altogether a free and happy people.

"Per order:
"Joseph Warren, *President, P. T.*"

NAMES OF THE KILLED AND WOUNDED AT LEXINGTON (p. 120) AND CONCORD.

The following list of the names of those first martyrs in the cause of American liberty is given in the eighteenth volume of the "Massachusetts Historical Collections:"—

Lexington.—*Killed*: Jonas Parker, Robert Monroe, Samuel Hadley, Jonathan Harrington, jr., Isaac Muzzy, Caleb Harrington, John Brown, Jedediah Moore, John Raymond, Nathaniel Wyman, 10. *Wounded*: John Robbins, Solomon Pierce, John Tidd, Joseph Comee, Ebenezer Monroe, jr., Thomas Winship, Nathaniel Farmer, Prince Estabrook, Jedediah Monroe, Francis Brown, 10.

Concord.—*Wounded*: Charles Miles, Nathan Barrett, Abel Prescott, jr., Jonas Brown, George Meriot, 5.

Cambridge.—*Killed*: William Marcy, Moses Richardson, John Hicks, Jason Russell, Jabez Wyman, Jason Winship, 6. *Wounded*: Samuel Whittemore, 1. *Missing*: Samuel Frost, Seth Russell, 2.

Needham.—*Killed*: John Bacon, Elisha Mills, Amos Mills, Nathaniel Chamberlain, Jonathan Parker, 5. *Wounded*: Eleazer Kingsbury, — — Tolman, 2.

Sudbury.—*Killed*: Josiah Haynes, Asahel Reed, 2. *Wounded*: Joshua Haynes, jr., 1.

Acton.—*Killed*: Isaac Davis, Abner Hosmer, James Hayward, 3. *Wounded*: Luther Blanchard, 1.

Bedford. — *Killed*: Jonathan Wilson, 1. *Wounded*: Job Lane, 1.

Woburn. — *Killed*: Daniel Thompson, Asahel Porter, 2. *Wounded*: George Reed, Jacob Bacon, — — Johnson, 3.

Medford. — *Killed*: Henry Putnam, William Polly, 2. (p. 121)

Charlestown. — *Killed*: James Miller, Edward Barber, 2.

Watertown. — *Killed*: Joseph Coolidge, 1.

Framingham. — *Wounded*: Daniel Heminway, 1.

Dedham. — *Killed*: Elias Haven, 1. *Wounded*: Israel Everett, 1.

Stowe. — *Wounded*: Daniel Conant, 1.

Roxbury. — *Missing*: Elijah Seaver, 1.

Brookline. — *Killed*: Isaac Gardner, 1.

Billerica. — *Wounded*: John Nichols, Timothy Blanchard, 2.

Chelmsford. — *Wounded*: Aaron Chamberlain, Oliver Barron, 2.

Salem. — *Killed*: Benjamin Pierce, 1.

Newton. — *Wounded*: Noah Wiswell, 1.

Danvers. — *Killed*: Henry Jacobs, Samuel Cook, Ebenezer Goldthwait, George Southwick, Benjamin Deland, Jotham Webb, Perley Putnam, 7. *Wounded*: Nathan Putnam, Dennis Wallace, 2. *Missing*: Joseph Bell, 1.

Beverly. — *Killed*: Reuben Kerryme, 1. *Wounded*: Nathaniel Cleves, Samuel Woodbury, William Dodge, 3.

Lynn. — *Killed*: Abednego Ramsdell, Daniel Townsend, William Flint, Thomas Hadley, 4. *Wounded*: Joshua Felt, Timothy Monroe, 2. *Missing*: Josiah Breed, 1.

Total: Killed, 49; Wounded, 39; Missing, 5 = 93.

A CATALOGUE
(p. 122)of
REVOLUTIONARY ARTICLES
in
THE POUGHKEEPSIE MUSEUM.

The following are among the Collection of Curiosities in the Museum at Poughkeepsie:—

original manuscripts.

Letter of Washington to Governor Clinton, acquainting him of a design of the British to seize his person while residing at Poughkeepsie, and convey him to New York. Dated at Dobbs's Ferry, 1780.

Letter of Washington to Brigadier-General Whiten on the subject of the removal of the troops from Trenton to Philadelphia. Dated Plumpton Plains, New Jersey, 1777.

Letter of Washington on the subject of promotions in the army. Dated 1779.

Note of invitation from Washington to Dr. John Thomas to dinner. Dr. Thomas was surgeon of the Massachusetts line. Dated headquarters, Newburgh, 1780.

Soldiers' (p. 123) discharge, signed by Washington, 1782.

Letter of the Marquis de Lafayette on the subject of fortifying the North river. Written to Governor Clinton in 1778.

Letter of the Baron Steuben to Governor Clinton on the good appearance of the New York line of the army. Dated New Windsor, 1780.

Letter of Lord Stirling to Governor Clinton on the discharge of the command of Major Wessenfells. Dated Albany, 1782.

Letter of Clinton in reply.

Resolution drawn up in Congress, and signed by John Hancock, requesting the state of New York to erect a monument, at continental expense, to the memory of Brigadier-General Herkimer, killed on the Mohawk in 1777. Dated in Congress, 1777.

Letter of Captain Abraham Schenck, of Fishkill, containing an order for old linen rags, for lint, for the surgeon of his command. Dated near Croton, 1776.

Letter of General Heath relating to beacons in the highlands. Dated Robintson's House, 1780.

Letter of General Heath on the condition of the prisoners confined in the Provost prison, at West Point. Dated Highlands, 1780.

Letter of Captain Nathaniel Toms, describing a chase after the British over the Schuylkill in 1777.

Journal of Lemuel Lyon, of Woodstock, Vermont, who served in the French and Indian war, in the expedition against Ticonderoga, commanded by General Abercrombie. The journal commences on the 5th of April, 1758, and closes on the 16th of November, 1759.

Journal (p. 124) of Samuel Haws, one of the minute-men called out on the day of the battle of Lexington: commencing April 19, 1775, and ending in January, 1776.

Three original letters of Washington to Colonel Marinus Willet, relating to a secret expedition against Oswego in 1782. Dated at Newburgh headquarters, 1782.

Letter of Joshua H. Smith, the person who conducted André toward the British lines. Directed from Goshen jail to Governor Clinton, complaining of the state of his health and the closeness of his confinement. Dated 1780.

Letter of Ezekiel Hyatt, of Crompond, Westchester county, to James Jackson, Esq., of Fishkill, in Dutchess county, informing him that Husson, a notorious cowboy and freebooter, had gone up to steal his horses, and was to have a hundred guineas if he got them. Dated Crompond, 1777.

Letter of Lieutenant Lawrence on the subject of the departure of the British fleet from the harbor of Newport. Dated Reading, 1780.

Letter by the direction of Washington to Abraham Schenck and others, of Fishkill, to solicit shirts of the inhabitants of their precinct for the soldiers of the army, many of whom were utterly destitute of that article. Dated Kingston, 1780.

Letter of Samuel Barker, while confined in the Provost prison, New York, to his wife in Westchester county. Dated Provost Prison, 1777.

miscellaneous articles.

Lock of Washington's hair — an unquestionable relic — derived from the late Judge Thompson, of the supreme court of the (p. 125) United States. Presented by his recent widow, the present Mrs. Lansing, of Poughkeepsie.

Fragments of the first coffin of Washington. Presented by Lewis Grube, Esq., artist, Poughkeepsie.

One of the points of the *chevaux-de-frieze* placed in the Hudson river, near New Windsor, in 1780, to prevent the passage of the British ships. It was raised accidentally by the anchor of a sloop commanded by Captain Abraham Elting, in New Paltiz, Ulster county, in 1836. It is pointed with iron, and weighs some hundreds of pounds.

Wooden camp candlestick, used in General Smallwood's brigade while encamped at Fishkill, in Dutchess county, in the Revolution. From Jackson Diddle, Esq., Fishkill.

Homespun linen rifle-shirt, worn by Captain Abraham Duryea at the battle of Long Island. From Charles Robinson, Esq., Fishkill.

Sheet of stamp-parchment, containing the stamps and duties of the stamp-act.

Sword of Captain Archibald Campbell, killed at the skirmish at Ward's house, in Weschester county, in 1776. Captain Campbell was the commanding officer of the British party. From his grandson, Captain Archibald Campbell, of Pawlings, Dutchess county.

Sword of one of Lee's legion, of Virginia. It has inscribed, on one side of the blade, "Victory or Death!" — on the opposite side, "Grenadiers of Virginia."

Tooth of Miss Jane M'Crea, found lying in her coffin when her remains were disinterred and removed to Fort Edward in 1824, by

Mr. George Barker, of Sandy Hill, and presented by him (p. 126) to the late Captain Matthew Danvers, of Sandy Hill, and to the collection by his widow, Mrs. Mary Danvers, of Poughkeepsie.

Iron-pipe tomahawk, found on the battle-field of Saratoga. From Van Wyck Brinkerhoff, Esq., of Fishkill.

Cannon-rammer, taken with Burgoyne at Saratoga. Purchased, with a lot of other "lumber" (sold at West Point by order of the government, after the Revolution), by Joseph Jackson, Esq., and others, of Fishkill. From Van Wyck Brinkerhoff, Esq., of Fishkill.

Knapsack of Captain David Uhl, a captain of militia in the Revolution, and worn by him when he joined his regiment at Harlem, in 1776. It is made of homespun linen. From his daughter, Mrs. Henry Abell, of Union Vale, Dutchess county.

Hessian camp-kettle, dug up on the battle-field of Bennington. By Mr. Charles Hoag, of Dover, Dutchess county.

Iron spur, found on the battle-field of the Cowpens. It is much rusted, and is believed to have belonged to one of Tarleton's men. From B. J. Lossing, Esq., of Poughkeepsie.

United States musket, found on the line of the retreat of the Americans from the battle-ground at Hubbardton, Vermont. It has the date of 1774 on the breech. From B. J. Lossing, Esq.

Collection of relics from all the battle-fields of the Revolution. From B. J. Lossing, Esq.

Cocked hat, worn by Lemuel Lyon on board the tea-ship in Boston harbor. The wearer was the writer of the first Journal in this volume. From his relative, Mr. J. Colby, of New York city.

Surgical (p. 127) instruments of Dr. John Thomas, a regimental surgeon in the Revolution. They were used in several of the principal battles of the war. From his son, Mr. Thomas, of Poughkeepsie.

Original portrait of Dr. John Thomas.

Broken United States bayonet, found on the battle-ground of Guilford Courthouse, North Carolina. By Mr. Charles Ney, of Amenia, Dutchess county.

Bayonet of John Woodin, a continental soldier. The point of this instrument was broken off in the wall of the fort at Stony Point, when in the body of a British soldier. Presented by a relative.

A Spanish dollar, taken from the cavity of the hip-bone of a skeleton dug up at Bemis's heights, Saratoga, in 1841. With it were five other dollars and an English guinea, and also a fragment of leather, supposed to be the remains of a purse or pocket-book. From Mrs. John Wing, of Washington, Dutchess county.

English musket, taken in a skirmish from a foraging-party of the British in Westchester county, in the Revolution, by Captain Abraham Meriot, of Newcastle, Westchester county, commander of a party of American militia. From Mr. John Townsend, of Poughkeepsie.

Tory musket, hidden during the whole period of the Revolution, in a hollow tree, in Dover, Dutchess county, to prevent its being seized by the committee-men and used against the king.

English musket, brought off from the battle-field of White Plains by Colonel Abraham Humphrey, of Smallwood's brigade. Presented by the late Colonel Humphrey Cornell, of Beekman, Dutchess county.

Fragments (p. 128) of human-bones from the battle-field of Red Bank. From B. J. Lossing, Esq., of Poughkeepsie.

Piece of one of the palmetto-logs of old Fort Moultrie, in Charleston harbor. From B. J. Lessing, Esq.

Horn of Lieutenant Charles Wallace, of the 1st Royal Highland regiment, curiously engraved with the names and distances of all the fortified posts from Quebec to Albany, together with the name and rank of the wearer. It was obtained from an Indian after the battle of Saratoga.

Metal button, ploughed up on Quaker hill, Dutchess county, where a division of the American array encamped in the Revolution. It has the letters "U. S. A." raised on the surface. A number of other articles belonging to the camp have been found in the neighborhood. A long line of the stone fireplaces of the soldiers still remain.

Spontoon of Lieutenant Alfred Van Wyck, of Fishkill, Dutchess county, used in hunting the cowboys in Fishkill mountain, in the Revolution. By his son, Theodorus Van Wyck, Esq., of Fishkill Hook, who remembers to have been shown, within the last forty years, by an individual then living, the bones of a "skinner," or cowboy, still lying unburied in a defile of the mountains.

==> Also, a large collection of other curiosities.

THE END.

Footnote 1: Canada expedition.(Back)

Footnote 2: Landlord. The proprietor of an inn or tavern was universally called *landlord.* The title is still very prevalent.(Back)

Footnote 3: To take carts for the military service. Under martial law, any private property may be used for the public good. A just government always pays a fair price for the same.(Back)

Footnote 4: Probably General Lyman, who was the commander-in-chief of the Connecticut forces at that time.(Back)

Footnote 5: In Litchfield county, Connecticut.(Back)

Footnote 6: Cornwall.(Back)

Footnote 7: Canaan.(Back)

Footnote 8: Livingston's manor, in Columbia county. The estates of Livingston, Van Rensselaer, and others, who received grants of land from government, on certain conditions, in order to encourage immigration and agriculture, were called Patroon Lands, and the proprietors were entitled Patroons, or patrons.(Back)

Footnote 9: Kinderhook.(Back)

Footnote 10: Now East Albany, on the east side of the Hudson river.(Back)

Footnote 11: Schenectady.(Back)

Footnote 12: Billeting-money — that is, money to pay for lodgings at private houses. When soldiers are quartered at private houses, it is said that such ones are *billeted* at such a house, &c.(Back)

Footnote 13: Schenectady.(Back)

Footnote 14: Alarum, or alarm.(Back)

Footnote 15: Schenectady.(Back)

Footnote 16: Provincial troops, or American soldiers. The English troops were called regulars.(Back)

Footnote 17: Massachusetts Bay troops. The Massachusetts colony was called *Massachusetts Bay* until after the War for Independence.(Back)

Footnote 18: Fort Edward was situated upon the east bank of the Hudson, about fifty miles north of Albany. The fort was built by General Lyman, of Connecticut, in 1755, while that officer was encamped there with about six thousand troops, awaiting the arrival of General William Johnson, the commander-in-chief of the expedition against the French at Ticonderoga and Crown Point. A portion of the site of the fort is now (1854) occupied by the flourishing village of Fort Edward. Some of the embankments are yet visible near the river. It was near this fort that Jane McCrea was killed and scalped, in 1777.(Back)

Footnote 19: Near Waterford, on the west side of the Hudson river, thirteen miles north from Albany.(Back)

Footnote 20: Niskayuna, a short distance from Waterford, and remarkable as a settlement of Shaking Quakers.(Back)

Footnote 21: On the Mohawk, about five miles above Cohoes Falls. It was the chief crossing-place for troops on their way north from Albany. There the right wing of the American army, under Arnold, was encamped, while General Schuyler was casting up entrenchments at Cohoes Falls, a few weeks before the Saratoga battles, in 1777.(Back)

Footnote 22: Stillwater is on the west bank of the Hudson, in Saratoga county, twenty-four miles north from Albany. The battle of Bemis's heights was fought near there, in 1777, and is sometimes known as the battle of Stillwater. Opposite the mouth of the Hoosick river, at Stillwater, was a stockade, called Fort Winslow.(Back)

Footnote 23: A batteau is a kind of scow or flat-boat, used on shallow streams like the Hudson above Waterford.(Back)

Footnote 24: Saratoga. This settlement was near the mouth of the Fish creek, on the south side. The village of Schuylerville is just across the stream, on the north side. On the plain, in front of the village of Schuylerville, was a regular quadrangular fortification, with bastions, called Fort Hardy. It was erected in 1756, and named in honor of the governor of New York at that time.(Back)

Footnote 25: On the west side of the Hudson, six or eight miles below Fort Edward. The river is there broken by swift rapids. During this campaign, Major (afterward General) Putnam was here surprised by a party of Indians, and boldly descended the rapids in a canoe, and escaped. It was a feat they never dared to attempt, and they felt certain that he was under the protection of the Great Spirit. Here a stream called Bloody Run enters the Hudson. It is so named because a party of soldiers from the garrison, in 1759, went there to fish, were surprised by the Indians, and nine were killed and scalped.(Back)

Footnote 26: Lake George.(Back)

Footnote 27: Fever-and-ague.(Back)

Footnote 28: Fitch's.(Back)

Footnote 29: Afterward called Snook's creek. It enters the Hudson three miles below Fort Edward.(Back)

Footnote 30: General Phineas Lyman, who built Fort Edward. He was a native of Durham, Connecticut, where he was born in 1716. He completed his education at Yale college, and afterward became an eminent lawyer. He was appointed commander-in-chief of the Connecticut forces in 1755, and in the expedition to Lake George deserved all the honor awarded to General Johnson, who was jealous of Lyman's abilities as a soldier. Lyman did his duty nobly, and was but little noticed. Johnson was unfit for his station, but being a nephew of Sir Peter Warren, then a popular English admiral, he received the honor of knighthood, and the sum of twenty thousand dollars, for his services in that campaign! General Lyman served with distinction until the close of the campaign in 1760, and in 1762 commanded the American forces sent against Havana. He was in England about eleven years, and, after his return, went with his family to the Mississippi, where he died in 1788.(Back)

Footnote 31: Colonel David Wooster, of Connecticut, the eminent general of the Revolution, who was killed at Ridgefield, while engaged in the pursuit of Tryon, after the burning of Danbury, in the spring of 1777. He was born in Stratford, Connecticut, in March, 1710, graduated at Yale college in 1738, and soon afterward received the appointment of captain of a vessel of the coast-guard. He was in the expedition against Louisburg in 1745. He afterward went to England, where he was a favorite at the court of George II., and received the appointment of captain in the regular service, under Sir

William Pepperell. He was promoted to a colonelcy in 1755, and rose to the rank of brigadier before the close of the French and Indian war. He was one of the most active men in getting up the expedition against Ticonderoga, in 1775, which resulted in the capture of that fortress, and also Crown Point, by Colonel Ethan Allen and Benedict Arnold. Wooster was appointed one of the first brigadiers of the continental army, in 1775, and third in rank. He was also appointed the first major-general of the militia of his state, when organized for the War for Independence; and in that capacity he was employed, with Arnold, Silliman, and others, in repelling British invasion in 1777. He lost his life in that service. His remains were buried at Danbury; and in 1854 a monument was erected over his grave by his grateful countrymen, at the expense of his native state.(Back)

Footnote 32: Chaplain.(Back)

Footnote 33: Commander of a corps of rangers, who performed signal services during the greater part of the French and Indian war. He was the son of an Irishman, an early settler of Dunbarton, in New Hampshire. He was appointed to his command in 1755, and was a thorough scout. In 1759, he was sent by General Amherst to destroy the Indian village of St. Francis. In that expedition he suffered great hardships, but was successful. He served in the Cherokee war in 1761, and in 1766 was appointed governor of Michilimacinac, where he was accused of treason, and sent to Montreal in irons. He was acquitted, went to England, and, after suffering imprisonment for debt, returned to America, where he remained until the Revolution broke out. He took up arms for the king, and in 1777 went to England, where he died. His "Journal of the French and Indian War" is a valuable work.(Back)

Footnote 34: Israel Putnam, afterward the Revolutionary general. He was born in Salem, Massachusetts, in January, 1718. He was a vigorous lad, and in 1739 we find him cultivating land in Pomfret, Connecticut, the scene of his remarkable adventure in a wolf's den, so familiar to every reader. He was appointed to the command of some of the first troops raised in Connecticut for the French and Indian war in 1755, and was an active officer during the entire period of that conflict, especially while in command of a corps of rangers. He was ploughing in his field when the news of the skirmishes at Lexington and Concord reached him. He immediately started for Boston, and, at the head of Connecticut troops, was active in the battle of Bunker Hill. He was one of the first four major-generals of the continental army appointed by Congress in June, 1775, and he was constantly on duty in important movements until 1779, when a partial paralysis of one side of his body disabled him for military service. He lived in retirement after the war, and died at Brooklyn, Windham county, Connecticut, on the 29th of May, 1790, at the age of seventy-two years.(Back)

Footnote 35: General James Abercrombie, the commander-in-chief of the campaign. He was descended from an ancient Scotch family, and, because of signal services on the continent, was promoted to the rank of major-general, the military art having been his profession since boyhood. He was superseded by Lord Amherst, after his defeat at Ticonderoga, and returned to England in the spring of 1759.(Back)

Footnote 36: Sabbath-day Point. This is a fertile little promontory, jutting out into Lake George from the western shore, a few miles from the little village of Hague, and surrounded by the most picturesque scenery imaginable. It was so named, at this time, because it was early on Sunday morning that Abercrombie and his army left this place and proceeded down the lake. There a small provincial force had a desperate fight with a party of French and Indians, in 1756, and defeated them. Abercrombie's army went down the lake in batteaux and whaleboats, and reached the Point just at dark. Captain (afterward General) Stark relates that he supped with the young lord Howe that evening, at the Point, and that the nobleman made many anxious inquiries about the strength of Ticonderoga, the country to be traversed, &c., and, by his serious demeanor, evinced a presentiment of his sad fate. He was killed in a skirmish with a French scout two days afterward. His body was conveyed to Albany, in charge of Captain (afterward General) Philip Schuyler, and buried there. He was a brother of the admiral and general of that name, who commanded the British naval and land forces in America in 1776.(Back)

Footnote 37: "The order of march," says Major Rogers, "exhibited a splendid military show." There were sixteen thousand well-armed troops. Lord Howe, in a large boat, led the van of the flotilla, accompanied by a guard of rangers and expert boatmen. The regular troops occupied the centre, and the provincials the wings. The sky was clear and starry, and not a breeze ruffled the dark waters as they slept quietly in the shadows of the mountains. Their oars were muffled, and, so silently did they move on, that not a scout upon the hills observed them; and the first intimation that the outposts of the enemy received of their approach was the full blaze of their scarlet uniforms, when, soon after sunrise, they landed and pushed on toward Ticonderoga.(Back)

Footnote 38: Rapids in the stream which forms the outlet of Lake George into Lake Champlain. Here are now extensive saw and grist mills. The distance from the foot of Lake George to Fort Ticonderoga is about four miles.(Back)

Footnote 39: The English lacked suitable guides, and became bewildered in the dense forest that covered the land. Lord Howe was second in command, and led the van, preceded by Major Putnam and a scout of one hundred men, to reconnoitre. The French set fire to their own outpost, and retreated. Howe and Putnam dashed on through the woods, and in a few minutes fell in with the French advanced guard, who were also bewildered, and were trying to find their way to the fort. A smart skirmish ensued, and, at the first fire, Lord Howe, another officer, and several privates, were killed. The French were repulsed, with a loss of about three hundred killed, and one hundred and forty made prisoners. The English battalions were so much broken, confused, and fatigued, that Abercrombie ordered them back to the landing-place, where they bivouacked for the night.(Back)

Footnote 40: This was Abercrombie's fatal mistake. He sent an engineer to reconnoitre the fort and outworks. The engineer reported the latter to be so weak, in an unfinished state, as to be easily carried, without artillery, by the force of English bayonets. The difficulties in the way of heavy cannons, in that dense forest, were very formidable; and Abercrombie was willing to rely upon sword and bayonet, on the strength of his engineer's report. That functionary

86

was mistaken; and when the English approached the French lines, they found an embankment of earth and stones, eight feet in height, strongly guarded by *abatis*, or felled trees, with their tops outward. The English made a furious attack, cut pathways through these prostrate trees, and mounted the parapet. They were instantly slain, and thus scores of Britons were sacrificed, by discharges of heavy cannons. When two thousand men had fallen, Abercrombie sounded a retreat, and the whole British army made its way to the landing-place at the foot of Lake George, with a loss of twenty-five hundred muskets. They went up the lake to Fort William Henry, and the wounded were sent to Fort Edward and to Albany. At his own solicitation, Colonel Bradstreet was sent to attack the French fort Frontenac, where Kingston now stands, at the foot of Lake Ontario; and General Stanwix proceeded to erect a fort toward the head-waters of the Mohawk, where the village of Rome now flourishes.(Back)

Footnote 41: The head of the lake was especially designated as "Lake George." There was the dilapidated fort William Henry, built by Sir William Johnson, in the autumn of 1755; and, about half a mile southeast from it, Fort George was afterward erected. The ruins of its citadel may yet (1854) be seen.(Back)

Footnote 42: Pomeroy.(Back)

Footnote 43: Flogging was facetiously termed "putting on a new shirt." Seventy lashes was a pretty severe punishment.(Back)

Footnote 44: This was the outlet of three little lakes, situated about half way between the head of Lake George and the bend of the Hudson at Sandy Hill. They are the head-waters of Clear river, the west branch of Wood creek, which empties into Lake Champlain at Whitehall.(Back)

Footnote 45: This was Diamond island, lying directly in front of Dunham's bay, and not far from the village of Caldwell. It was so called because of the number and beauty of quartz-crystals found upon it. Burgoyne made it a depôt of military stores when on his way from Canada, by the way of Lake Champlain, in 1777. It was the scene of a sharp conflict between the little garrison and a party of Americans under Colonel Brown, on the 25th of September, 1777, while Gates and Burgoyne were confronted at Saratoga. Brown was repulsed.(Back)

Footnote 46: Partridge's.(Back)

Footnote 47: They were volunteers.(Back)

Footnote 48: M'Mahon?(Back)

Footnote 49: This locality can not be identified.(Back)

Footnote 50: Rogers, in his Journal, speaks of this occurrence. He says it was on the 27th, and that one hundred and sixteen men were killed, of whom sixteen were rangers.(Back)

Footnote 51: He went out with seven hundred men, to intercept the marauding party, but they escaped.(Back)

Footnote 52: Ingersoll.(Back)

Footnote 53: Rogers says that, on his return from his attempt to intercept the marauding party, he was met by an express, with orders to march toward the head of Lake Champlain, at South and East bays, to prevent the French marching upon Fort Edward. There he was joined by Major Putnam and Captain Dalyell or D'Ell.(Back)

Footnote 54: Packet.(Back)

Footnote 55: A severe engagement took place on Clear river, the west branch of Wood creek, about a mile northwest from Fort Anne village (then the site of a picketed blockhouse, called Fort Anne), between a party of rangers and provincials under Rogers, Putnam, and Captain Dalyell, or D'Ell, and about an equal number of French and Indians under Molang, a famous partisan leader. The English troops were marching when attacked: Putnam was in front, with the provincials; Rogers was in the rear, with his rangers; and D'Ell in the centre, with the regulars. Molang attacked them in front, and a powerful Indian rushed forward and made Putnam a prisoner. The provincials were thrown into great confusion, but were rallied by Lieutenant Durkee, who was one of the victims of the Wyoming massacre twenty years afterward. D'Ell, with Gage's light infantry, behaved very gallantly, and the rangers finally put the enemy to flight. The latter lost about two hundred men. Colonel Prevost, then in command at Fort Edward, sent out three hundred men, with refreshments for the party, and all arrived at Fort Edward on the

9th. This was the relief-party mentioned in the text, under date of the 8th.(Back)

Footnote 56: This is an island in the Hudson, opposite Fort Edward, and known as Rogers's island.(Back)

Footnote 57: Sutler's.(Back)

Footnote 58: Fitch.(Back)

Footnote 59: Ticonderoga.(Back)

Footnote 60: The Indian who seized Putnam tied him to a tree, and for a time he was exposed to the cross-fire of the combatants. His garments were riddled by bullets, but, strange to say, not one touched his person. He was carried away in the retreat, his wrists tightly bound with cords. The Indians rejoiced over the capture of their great enemy, and he was doomed to the torture. In the deep forest he was stripped naked, bound to a sapling, wood was piled high around him, the death-songs of the savages were chanted, and the torch was applied. Just then a heavy shower of rain almost extinguished the flames. They were again bursting forth with fiercer intensity, when a French officer, informed of what was going on, darted through the crowd of yelling savages, and released the prisoner. He was delivered to Montcalm at Ticonderoga, then sent to Montreal, and, after being treated kindly, was exchanged for a prisoner taken by Colonel Bradstreet at Frontenac.(Back)

Footnote 61: Picket.(Back)

Footnote 62: Fort Misery was a breastwork at the mouth of Moses's kill, or creek, a short distance from Fort Miller, on the east side of the Hudson.(Back)

Footnote 63: At Fort George, at the head of Lake George.(Back)

Footnote 64: Volleys.(Back)

Footnote 65: It was the king's birthday. The firing of twenty-one heavy guns formed a royal salute.(Back)

Footnote 66: Bridge.(Back)

Footnote 67: Fort Musquito was a breastwork cast up at the mouth of Snooks' creek.(Back)

Footnote 68: This was a nickname for the regular troops, who were dressed in scarlet uniforms.(Back)

Footnote 69: Wrestled.(Back)

Footnote 70: Fort Anne was erected in 1757, a year before the occurrences here narrated took place. It was a strong blockhouse of logs, with portholes for cannon and loopholes for musketry, and surrounded by a picket of pine-saplings. When the writer visited the spot in 1848, he dug up the part of one of the pickets yet remaining in the earth, and, on splitting it, it emitted the pleasant odor of a fresh pine-log, though ninety years had elapsed since it was placed there. This fort was near the bank of Wood creek, about eleven miles from the head of Lake Champlain, at the village of Whitehall. It was in the line of Burgoyne's march toward the Hudson, in 1777; and near it quite a severe skirmish took place between Colonel Long, of Schuyler's army, and a British detachment under Colonel Hill, on the 8th of July, the day after Ticonderoga was abandoned to the enemy. Victory was almost within the grasp of Colonel Long, when his ammunition failed, and he was compelled to retreat.(Back)

Footnote 71: Canoe.(Back)

Footnote 72: Fort Misery.(Back)

Footnote 73: The Indian name of the site of Fort Frontenac (where Kingston, Upper Canada, now stands), taken by Colonel Bradstreet, was Cataraqua. That was also the Indian name for Lake Ontario.(Back)

Footnote 74: Fascines—bundles of sticks, mixed with earth, and used for filling ditches in the construction of forts.(Back)

Footnote 75: Pomeroy.(Back)

Footnote 76: Militia.(Back)

Footnote 77: Pomeroy.(Back)

Footnote 78: The channel between Rogers's island, on which the great blockhouse was built, and Fort Edward, does not exceed two hundred feet in width.(Back)

Footnote 79: Christening.(Back)

Footnote 80: General Amherst.(Back)

Footnote 81: Amherst.(Back)

Footnote 82: Pomeroy.(Back)

Footnote 83: Halifax, Nova Scotia.(Back)

Footnote 84: Tomahawk.(Back)

Footnote 85: Scalped.(Back)

Footnote 86: British regular.(Back)

Footnote 87: A mixture of beer and rum, warmed by thrusting a hot iron into it.(Back)

Footnote 88: Hinman's.(Back)

Footnote 89: Prebles.(Back)

Footnote 90: Waiter.(Back)

Footnote 91: Sutler.(Back)

Footnote 92: The "third fall," as it was called, in the Hudson, at Sandy Hill.(Back)

Footnote 93: Reveillé.(Back)

Footnote 94: Provost.(Back)

Footnote 95: Hogeboom's.(Back)

Footnote 96: See note, page 13.(Back)

Footnote 97: Coventry.(Back)

Footnote 98: In Norfolk county, Massachusetts, thirty-two miles southwest from Boston.(Back)

Footnote 99: See introductory remarks. The skirmishes at Lexington and Concord occurred early in the morning of this day.(Back)

Footnote 100: See introductory remarks.(Back)

Footnote 101: Twenty-one miles from Boston.(Back)

Footnote 102: Thirteen miles from Boston.(Back)

Footnote 103: Colonel John Greaton. He was a bold officer, and commanded a corps which performed a sort of ranger service. At this time he was only a major. In June following he carried off about eight hundred sheep and lambs, and some cattle, from Deer island.

About that time he was promoted to the rank of colonel. In the middle of July, he led one hundred and thirty-six men, in whale-boats, to destroy forage and other property on Long island, in Boston harbor; and at one time he captured a barge belonging to a British man-of-war. In April, 1776, he accompanied General Thompson to Canada. He was promoted to the rank of brigadier in the continental army, in January, 1783.(Back)

Footnote 104: Jamaica Plain, six miles from Boston.(Back)

Footnote 105: The isthmus that connected the peninsula of Boston with the main, at Roxbury.(Back)

Footnote 106: The British soldiers were all called regulars. This word denotes soldiers belonging to the regular army, as distinguished from militia.(Back)

Footnote 107: Twelve miles southeast from Boston.(Back)

Footnote 108: One mile from Boston.(Back)

Footnote 109: Three miles northwest from Boston.(Back)

Footnote 110: Thirty-one miles southeast from Boston.(Back)

Footnote 111: Tories were those who adhered to the British. It is a name derived from the vocabulary of English politics in the time of Charles II. A *tory*, then, was an adherent of the crown; a *whig* was an opposer of the government. The word was first used in America about 1770.(Back)

Footnote 112: Twenty-one miles southwest from Boston.(Back)

Footnote 113: Rev. Amos Adams, a minister at Roxbury. He was a graduate of Harvard college. He died of dysentery, which prevailed in the camp, at Dorchester, on the 5th of October, 1775, in the forty-eighth year of his age.(Back)

Footnote 114: On Sunday morning, the 21st of May, the British commander sent two sloops and an armed schooner to take off a quantity of hay from Grape island. They were opposed by the people who gathered on the point nearest the island. These finally got two vessels afloat, went to the island, drove the British off, burnt eighty tons of hay, and brought off many cattle. There was some severe fighting during the affair. Mrs. John Adams, writing to her husband, said: "You inquire who were at the engagement at Grape island. I may say with truth, all of Weymouth, Braintree, and Hingham, who were able to bear arms.... Both your brothers were there; your younger brother with his company, who gained honor by their good order that day. He was one of the first to venture on board a schooner, to land upon the island." Mr. Adams was then in the Continental Congress, at Philadelphia.(Back)

Footnote 115: On Saturday, May 27th, a detachment of Americans was sent to drive all the live stock from Hog and Noddle's islands, near Boston. They were observed by the British, who despatched a sloop, a schooner, and forty marines, to oppose them. They were fired on from the vessels, and quite severe skirmishing continued through the night. The Americans sent for reinforcements, and, at about nine o'clock at night, some three hundred men and two pieces of cannon arrived, commanded by General Putnam in person, and accompanied by Dr. Warren as a volunteer. They compelled the British to abandon their sloop, and the Americans took possession of it. The British lost twenty killed and fifty wounded. The Americans had none killed, and only four wounded. They captured twelve swivels and four four-pound cannon, besides clothing and money.(Back)

Footnote 116: Noddle's.(Back)

Footnote 117: Probably the house of Joshua Loring, jr., near Roxbury, who was a violent loyalist. General Gage made him sole auctioneer in Boston. He was afterward commissary of prisoners in New York. His wife is referred to in Hopkinson's poem, *"The Battle of the Kegs."*(Back)

Footnote 118: Colonel John Robinson, who was second in command in the skirmish at Concord on the 19th of April. He commanded the detachment that guarded Boston neck, for some time. Speaking of that duty, Gordon remarks: "The colonel was obliged, therefore, for the time mentioned, to patrol the guards every night, which gave him a round of nine miles to traverse."(Back)

Footnote 119: Harlots.(Back)

Footnote 120: General Thomas, who had command of the right wing, extending from Roxbury to Dorchester. General Artemas

Ward was the commander-in-chief until the arrival of Washington, early in July.(Back)

Footnote 121: Fascines. See note on page 35.(Back)

Footnote 122: This is a mistake. It was Breed's hill, nearer Charlestown and Boston than Bunker's hill. Colonel William Prescott, and not General Putnam, was entrenched there, and was in command during the engagement. He had been sent with a company, the night before, about a thousand strong, to throw up a redoubt on Bunker's hill. He made a mistake, and performed the work on Breed's hill. The British had no suspicion of the work that went on during that sultry June night, and were greatly alarmed when they saw a formidable breastwork overlooking their shipping in the harbor, and menacing the city. During the engagement, General Putnam was on Bunker's hill, urging on reinforcements for Prescott. Dr. Warren, just appointed major-general, joined Prescott as a volunteer during the battle, and was mortally wounded just as the conflict ended. It must be remembered that the writer of this Journal was in General Thomas's division, which did not participate in the battle of the 17th of June.(Back)

Footnote 123: Prospect hill. The Americans retreated from Breed's and Bunker's hills to Winter and Prospect hills, and Cambridge. The remains of the American entrenchments on Prospect hill were demolished in 1817.(Back)

Footnote 124: Colonel James Reed, of New Hampshire. He was active in the battle of the 17th. He was a brave officer, and was at the head of a regiment at Ticonderoga the following year.(Back)

Footnote 125: The Americans were alarmed on the 24th by indications that the whole British army in Boston was about to force its way across Boston neck. At noon they commenced throwing bomb-shells into Roxbury, but the alert soldiers prevented damage from them, and saved the town. Colonel Miller, of Rhode Island, said in a letter—"Such was the courage of our men, that they would go and take up a burning carcass or bomb, and take out the fuse!"(Back)

Footnote 126: The house and barns of Thomas Brown were on the neck, about a mile from Roxbury meeting-house, and were occupied by the British advanced guard. Two Americans tried to set fire to the barn on the 24th, and were killed.(Back)

Footnote 127: The British again hurled some shells into Roxbury on Sunday, the 2d of July, but the extent of the damage was setting fire to one house, which was consumed.(Back)

Footnote 128: George Washington was chosen commander-in-chief of the continental armies on the 15th of June, 1775. He set out for the headquarters of the army at Cambridge on the 21st, reached there on the 2d of July, and took formal command of the army on the morning of the 3d.(Back)

Footnote 129: A party of volunteers, under Majors Tupper and Crane, attacked the British advanced guards, drove them in, and set fire to Brown's house. They took several muskets, and retreated without loss.(Back)

Footnote 130: It is impossible to identify this place. A letter, dated on the 12th, says, "We have just got, over land from Cape Cod, a large fleet of whaleboats," &c., &c. The place alluded to in the text was probably near Boston.(Back)

Footnote 131: This party went from Roxbury camp. The report says that they brought from Long island "fifteen prisoners, two hundred sheep, nineteen cattle, thirteen horses, and three hogs." The prisoners were taken to Concord.(Back)

Footnote 132: The party under Colonel Greaton, mentioned in a preceding note.(Back)

Footnote 133: Twenty miles south from Boston.(Back)

Footnote 134: A strong party of Americans took possession of an advanced post in Roxbury, upon which the British kept up an incessant fire.(Back)

Footnote 135: Upton is thirty-five miles southwest from Boston.(Back)

Footnote 136: The 20th was observed throughout the camps as a day of fasting and prayer. Before daylight that morning, a party from Heath's regiment landed on Nantasket point, set fire to the lighthouse, and brought away a thousand bushels of barley and a quantity of hay.(Back)

Footnote 137: This was a very strong quadrangular work, on the highest eminence in Roxbury. It had four bastions, and in every respect was a regular work. It is now well preserved, the embankments being from six to fifteen feet in height from without.(Back)

Footnote 138: On that day the British, five hundred strong, marched over the neck, and built a slight breastwork to cover their guard. The American camp was in alarm all the day, and that night the troops lay on their arms. The tories in Boston were also alarmed, for they dreaded an invasion of the city by their exasperated countrymen.(Back)

Footnote 139: Marines.(Back)

Footnote 140: The British commenced rebuilding the lighthouse on Nantasket point. Major Tupper, with three hundred men, attacked the working-party, killed ten or twelve men, and took the rest prisoners. He then demolished the works, but, before he could leave, some armed boats came to oppose him. In the skirmishing that ensued, fifty-three of the British were killed or captured. Tupper lost one man killed, and two wounded.(Back)

Footnote 141: A party of British troops sallied out toward Roxbury, drove in the American pickets, and burned the tavern which was situated upon the portion of the neck nearest Roxbury.(Back)

Footnote 142: When the British built their breastwork on the neck, the Sunday previous, they had a floating battery brought into Charles river, and moored it within three hundred yards of Sewall's point.(Back)

Footnote 143: The Brookline fort was on Sewall's point, between Roxbury and Cambridge. It commanded the entrance to Charles river.(Back)

Footnote 144: The village and church of Dorchester was four miles from Boston. The heights of Dorchester are in what is now called South Boston.(Back)

Footnote 145: Joseph Willard, D.D., who was made president of Harvard college in December, 1781. He died in New Bedford, in 1804, at the age of sixty-four years.(Back)

Footnote 146: A nickname given to the British regulars, on account of their red suits. They were so called in England, as early as the time of Queen Anne.(Back)

Footnote 147: The large park, known as Boston Common, extended down to the water's edge, before the flats were filled in.(Back)

Footnote 148: About nine o'clock on Sunday morning, the 27th, the British opened a heavy cannonade from Bunker's hill (where they had built a strong redoubt), and from a ship and floating battery in Mystic river. The firing was directed upon the American works on Winter, Prospect, and Ploughed hills. They continued to bombard these works daily until the 10th of September.(Back)

Footnote 149: There was a famous tree in Boston, under which the patriots had often held meetings since the time of the stamp-act excitement. On that account it was called "Liberty-Tree." It was a noble elm, and stood at the corner of the present Washington and Essex streets. On the 31st of August, 1775, the British cut it down, with no apparent motive but the indulgence of petty spite. An eye-witness of the event says: "After a long spell of laughing and grinning, sweating, swearing, and foaming, with malice diabolical, they cut down a tree, because it bore the name of liberty." A tory soldier was killed by its fall. A poet of the day wrote: —

"A tory soldier, on its topmost limb —
The Genius of the Shade looked stern at him,
And marked him out that same hour to dine
Where unsnuffed lamps burn low at Pluto's shrine.
Then tripped his feet from off their cautious stand:
Pale turned the wretch — he spread each helpless hand,
But spread in vain — with headlong force he fell,
Nor stopped descending till he stopped in hell!" (Back)

Footnote 150: Colonel Jedediah Huntington, of Norwich, Connecticut. The British now seemed determined to make a general assault upon the besiegers, and a heavy cannonade was opened simultaneously upon the Americans at Roxbury and in the vicinity of Cambridge.(Back)

Footnote 151: They threw up a slight breastwork a little in advance of their lines on the neck, and not far from the George tavern.(Back)

Footnote 152: Lamb's dam was between Roxbury and Dorchester. There the Americans completed a strong work on the 10th of September, and mounted four eighteen-pounders.(Back)

Footnote 153: Skirmish.(Back)

Footnote 154: We can not explain this local allusion.(Back)

Footnote 155: The breastworks in the thicket were the Roxbury lines of fortifications in advance of the fort.(Back)

Footnote 156: Mystic.(Back)

Footnote 157: The road leading from Roxbury across the neck into Boston.(Back)

Footnote 158: Captain Pond was from New Hampshire, and was an officer in Colonel Stark's regiment.(Back)

Footnote 159: From the vessels known as men-of-war.(Back)

Footnote 160: Coronation. George III. and his wife Charlotte were crowned on the 22d of September, 1761. It was always a holyday next to that of the king's birthday.(Back)

Footnote 161: Frothingham says: "On the 23d, the British discharged one hundred and eight cannon and mortars on the works at Roxbury without doing any damage."(Back)

Footnote 162: This expedition was under Major Tupper. They burnt a fine pleasure-boat just ready to be launched, belonging to some British officers.(Back)

Footnote 163: Of the Rhode Island "Army of Observation," under General Greene.(Back)

Footnote 164: This was a sloop-of-war, carrying twenty guns.(Back)

Footnote 165: He probably refers to the prisoners taken in the armed schooner *Margaretta*, at Machias, Maine, in the month of May, by some Americans under Jeremiah O'Brien; or they may have been of the crew of two small cruisers afterward captured by O'Brien. They were taken to Watertown, where the Provincial Congress of Massachusetts was in session.(Back)

Footnote 166: The writer of this Journal.(Back)

Footnote 167: These riflemen were from Maryland. The company had been raised by order of Congress, and placed in command of Captain Michael Cresap, who, without a shadow of justice, was made to figure unfavorably in the celebrated speech attributed to Logan, the Mingo chief. Proof is abundant that the stain put upon the character of Cresap, by the speech of Logan from the pen of Jefferson, was unmerited. Captain Cresap was taken sick, and, at about the time here indicated, he started for home, but died at New York, on the 18th of October, 1775, at the age of thirty-three years. His remains yet lie buried in Trinity churchyard, a few feet from Broadway.(Back)

Footnote 168: Shooting at a mark, for liquor.(Back)

Footnote 169: Communications are thus had between belligerent armies. By common consent, as a rule of war, a person approaching one army from another, with a white flag, is respected as a neutral; and to "fire upon a flag," as the phrase is when the bearer is fired upon, is considered a great breach of faith and honor.(Back)

Footnote 170: The wives of officers often visited permanent camps, and formed pleasant social parties. Mrs. Washington visited her husband at Cambridge, while he remained there. She also spent a portion of the winter with him at Valley Forge, and likewise at Morristown.(Back)

Footnote 171: Newton, seven miles north from Boston.(Back)

Footnote 172: When Major Tupper destroyed the lighthouse on Nantasket point, he carried away all the furniture and the great lamp by which it was lighted.(Back)

Footnote 173: The creek referred to is Stony brook, northward from Roxbury fort.(Back)

Footnote 174: As early as July, 1775, Dr. Franklin had suggested the propriety of a political confederation of all the colonies, and the establishment of governmental relations with foreign powers, especially with France, which, it was well known, hated England. In

November of that year, Benjamin Harrison, Benjamin Franklin, Thomas Johnson, John Dickenson, and John Jay, were appointed a committee to open and carry on correspondence with foreign governments; and in March following, Silas Deane was appointed a special agent of Congress to the court of France. Rumors of such intentions appear to have reached the army, according to our Journalist, as early as the 24th of October, 1775.(Back)

Footnote 175: A very natural consequence.(Back)

Footnote 176: During the whole of October, affairs were very quiet, and no skirmish of importance occurred. The "Essex Gazette" of the 19th said, "Scarcely a gun has been fired for a fortnight." On the 4th, a small fleet, under Captain Mowatt, sailed from Boston harbor, and destroyed Falmouth (now Portland), Maine. On the 15th, a committee from Congress arrived, to consult with Washington concerning the future, and a reorganization of the army.(Back)

Footnote 177: On this day there was quite a severe skirmish occurred at Lechmere's point, now Cambridgeport.(Back)

Footnote 178: That is, a written permission from his commanding officer, to leave for a specified time.(Back)

Footnote 179: At that time leather breeches were much in vogue, because they were durable. The more costly ones of buckskin were worn only by officers.(Back)

Footnote 180: Late in October a new organization of the army took place, and enlistments for a certain term were commenced. Hitherto there had been great confusion in the matter. The army had gathered around Boston from sudden impulse, and it was continually changing. The excitement which had brought them together had in a measure subsided, and enlistments went on slowly. After a month's exertions, only five thousand names were enrolled; and Washington, lamenting the dearth of public spirit, almost despaired. Alluding to the selfishness exhibited in camp, he says: "Such stock-jobbing and fertility in all low arts, to obtain advantages of one kind and another, I never saw before, and pray God I may never witness again."(Back)

Footnote 181: Generalissimo.(Back)

Footnote 182: On the previous day, General Putnam, with a strong detachment, broke ground at Cobble hill, where the M'Lean Asylum now stands. The object was to erect batteries for the purpose of cannonading Boston. It was expected the British troops would sally out of the city and attack them, and that expectation caused Washington to issue the order for *all* the troops to be ready for action at a moment's warning.(Back)

Footnote 183: Frothingham says, "Two British sentinels came off in the night to the detachment" of General Putnam.(Back)

Footnote 184: This remark refers to several blots of ink which disfigure the page of his Journal on which he was writing.(Back)

Footnote 185: That was the British storeship *Nancy*, captured off Cape Anne, and carried into that harbor, by Captain John Manly, commander of the American armed schooner *Lee*, one of the six vessels fitted out at Boston under the direction of Washington, before Congress had yet taken any measures to establish a navy. So valuable were the stores of the *Nancy*, that Washington supposed General Howe would immediately make efforts to recover her, and he had an armed force sent to Cape Anne to secure them. There were two thousand muskets, one hundred thousand flints, thirty thousand round shot for one, six, and twelve pounders, over thirty thousand musket-shot, and a thirteen-inch brass mortar that weighed twenty-seven hundred pounds. The arrival of these produced great joy in the camp. Colonel Moylan, describing the scene, says: "Old Put [General Putnam] was mounted on the mortar, with a bottle of rum in his hand, standing parson to christen, while godfather Mifflin [afterward General Mifflin] gave it the name of *Congress*."

On the 29th of November, Washington commenced planting a bomb-battery on Lechmere's point, with the intention of bombarding the British works on Bunker hill. They completed it in the course of a few days, entirely unmolested.(Back)

Footnote 186: The author did not expect to have his Journal published, or he would have omitted the entry here made. There seems nothing in it derogatory to his character, yet he has chosen words to express his thoughts not suited "to ears polite."(Back)

Footnote 187: Washington was now in hourly expectation of an attack from the British, and, knowing his own weakness, he considered his situation very critical. In vigilance alone seemed a security for safety.(Back)

Footnote 188: The Yankee love of trade and barter appears to have been very prevalent in the camp.(Back)

Footnote 189: New militia recruits from the country, who had never seen service.(Back)

Footnote 190: General Joseph Spencer, of East Haddam, Connecticut. He remained in service until 1778, when he resigned, left the army, and became a member of Congress. He held rank next to Putnam in the army at Boston. He died in 1789, at the age of seventy years.(Back)

Footnote 191: Cobble.(Back)

Footnote 192: These, it is said, were the most perfect of any of the fortifications raised around Boston at that time.(Back)

Footnote 193: Seven miles northwest from Boston. It was then the seat of the revolutionary government in Massachusetts.(Back)

Footnote 194: Washington issued a notice, on the 28th of October, that tailors would be employed to make coats for those who wished them.(Back)

Footnote 195: This was a mistake. On the 13th of September, Colonel Benedict Arnold left Cambridge with a detachment to cross the country by the way of the Kennebec, to invade Canada and capture Quebec. Arnold's army suffered terribly on the march, and arrived at Point Levi, opposite Quebec, on the 9th of November, and prepared to attack the city. He was obliged to postpone his attack, and Quebec never fell into the hands of the patriots.(Back)

Footnote 196: Lechmere's.(Back)

Footnote 197: A nickname given to Bunker's hill.(Back)

Footnote 198: On the night of the 28th, an unsuccessful attempt was made to surprise the British outposts on Charlestown neck, and then to attack the enemy on Bunker's hill. The Americans started to cross from Cobble hill, on the ice. One of the men slipped and fell when they were half way across, and his gun went off. This alarmed the British, and they were on their guard. It was computed that, from the burning of Charlestown, on the 17th of June, until Christmas day, the British had fired more than two thousand shot and shells. They hurled more than three hundred bombshells at Plowed hill, and one hundred at Lechmere's point. Gordon says that, with all this waste of metal, they "killed only seven men on the Cambridge side, and just a dozen on the Roxbury side."(Back)

Footnote 199: Anno Domini.(Back)

Footnote 200: Fascines.(Back)

Footnote 201: Delightfully.(Back)

Footnote 202: When Charlestown was burned, fourteen houses escaped the flames. These were occupied by the British; and, on the 8th of January, General Putnam sent Major Knowlton (afterward killed at Harlem), with a small party, to set those houses on fire. The affair was injudiciously managed, and, before all could be fired, the flames of one alarmed the British in the fort. They discharged cannons and small-arms in all directions, in their confusion and affright. At that moment a play, called "The Blockade of Boston," written for the occasion by General Burgoyne, was in course of performance in the city. In the midst of the scene in which Washington was burlesqued, a sergeant dashed into the theatre and exclaimed, "The Yankees are attacking Bunker's hill!" The audience thought it was part of the play, until General Howe said, "Officers, to your alarm-posts!" Then women shrieked and fainted, and the people rushed to the streets in great confusion.(Back)

Footnote 203: Sir James Wallace commanded a small British flotilla in Narraganset bay, during the summer and autumn of 1775. He was really a commissioned pirate, for he burnt and plundered dwellings, and stores, and plantations, wherever he pleased. The fact above alluded to was the plunder and destruction of the houses on the beautiful island of Providence (not the town of Providence) by that marauder, at the close of November, 1775. He also desolated Connanicut island, opposite Newport; and every American vessel that entered that harbor was seized and sent to Boston.(Back)

Footnote 204: Arnold, with only seven hundred men, appeared before Quebec on the 18th of November, and demanded its surrender. He was soon compelled to retire, and, marching up the St. Lawrence twenty miles, he there met, in December, General Montgomery, with a small force, descending from Montreal. They marched against Quebec, and, early in the morning of the 31st of December, proceeded to assail the city at three distinct points. Montgomery was killed, Morgan and many of the Americans were made prisoners, and Arnold, who was severely wounded, retired to Sillery, three miles above Quebec.(Back)

Footnote 205: Several of the prizes captured by Manly and others contained powder and arms; and late in December, Colonel (afterward General) Knox arrived from Ticonderoga with forty-two sled-loads of cannons, mortars, lead, balls, flints, &c. By the close of January, powder became quite plentiful in the American camp.(Back)

Footnote 206: Militia-men.(Back)

Footnote 207: Here the Journal ends abruptly, and we have no clew to the writer afterward. As he had enlisted for the campaign of 1776, he doubtless remained with the army until after the expulsion of the British from Boston, in March following, unless he was killed in some of the skirmishes that frequently occurred, or was obliged to leave the army on account of sickness. Whatever was his fate, the veil of oblivion is drawn over it, for he was one of the thousands who with warm hearts and stout hands struggled in the field for the liberties of their country, lie in unhonored graves, and have had no biographers. If he lived until the conflict ended, and died in his native town, no doubt his grave is in the old churchyard at Wrentham. His family was among the earliest settlers there, for Daniel Haws was a resident of the village when it was burnt, in the time of King Philip's war, almost two hundred years ago; and on a plain slab in that old burial-place is the name of Ebenezer Haws, who died in 1812, at the age of ninety-one years.(Back)